EXPLORERS
OF THE
RENAISSANCE

THE RENAISSANCE

c.l

EXPLORERS
OF THE
RENAISSANCE

Edited by Robert Curley , Senior Editor, Science and Technology

Britannica
Educational Publishing

IN ASSOCIATION WITH

ROSEN
EDUCATIONAL SERVICES

Published in 2013 by Britannica Educational Publishing
(a trademark of Encyclopædia Britannica, Inc.) in association with Rosen Educational Services, LLC
29 East 21st Street, New York, NY 10010.

Distributed exclusively by Rosen Educational Services.
For a listing of additional Britannica Educational Publishing titles, call toll free (800) 237-9932.

First Edition

Britannica Educational Publishing
J.E. Luebering: Senior Manager
Adam Augustyn: Assistant Manager
Marilyn L. Barton: Senior Coordinator, Production Control
Steven Bosco: Director, Editorial Technologies
Lisa S. Braucher: Senior Producer and Data Editor
Yvette Charboneau: Senior Copy Editor
Kathy Nakamura: Manager, Media Acquisition
Robert Curley: Senior Editor, Science and Technology

Rosen Educational Services
Jeanne Nagle: Senior Editor
Nelson Sá: Art Director
Cindy Reiman: Photography Manager
Brian Garvey: Designer, Cover Design
Introduction by Richard Barrington

Library of Congress Cataloging-in-Publication Data

Explorers of the Renaissance/edited by Robert Curley.
    p. cm.—(The Renaissance)
"In association with Britannica Educational Publishing, Rosen Educational Services."
Includes bibliographical references and index.
ISBN 978-1-61530-879-8 (library binding)
1. Explorers—Juvenile literature. 2. Discoveries in geography—Juvenile literature.
I. Curley, Robert, 1955-
G175.E965 2013
910.92'24—dc23

2012015599

Manufactured in the United States of America

CONTENTS

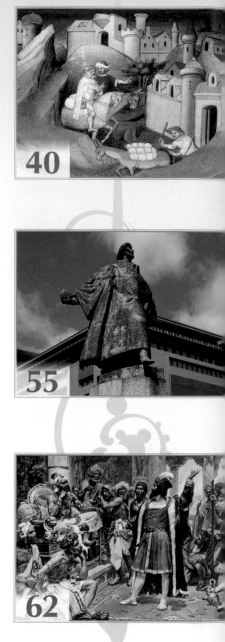

Chapter 5: Other Westward Navigators 92

Chapter 6: Monarchs and Sponsors 115

INTRODUCTION

The Renaissance is known as a time of tremendous artistic and intellectual achievement, but the accomplishments of the era were not solely triumphs of the mind. Great physical courage and stamina were needed by the explorers of the era, who stepped or sailed into the unknown to expand the boundaries of world knowledge. In detailing the achievements of explorers during what is known as the Age of Discovery, this book tells the story of that era; it is to be as much a tale of action and adventure as it is of the mind and spirit.

Though this story played out some 500 or more years ago, there are elements to it that are easily recognizable today. Religious and political tensions, technology, and commerce all fueled the progression of exploration throughout the Age of Discovery. Overland routes from Europe to Asia gave way to the development of seaborne eastward routes, which then led to westward exploration by sea in an attempt to reach Asia by circling around the far side of the world.

Religious conflict was an important spark to this progression, as the emergence of the Muslim Ottoman empire made overland routes to China and the court of Kublai Khan increasingly perilous for Christian European travelers and traders. Indeed, converting the great Khan and his Mongol empire to Christianity was a goal of some early Renaissance expeditions to east Asia. However, politics also played a hand, first when the breakup of the Mongol empire further increased the risks of overland travel to the region, and later when European nations jostled for the upper hand in exploring, trading with, and ultimately conquering new lands.

As for technology, its role was largely manifested in the development of navigational and shipbuilding techniques throughout this period. Until the Renaissance, navigation had progressed little since the time of Ptolemy in the second century CE. During the Renaissance, more ambitious exploration by sea took advantage of, and ultimately accelerated because of, navigational advancements. While basic navigation may not be thought of as high technology by modern standards, for its time it may be considered comparable to the Internet and air travel, regarding how it facilitated commerce and movement, and even to space exploration in that an element of the unknown was involved.

Commerce also was a constant driver behind the Age of Discovery. This was the case from the first wave of Renaissance exploration, which included the journeys of Marco Polo and a multitude of other great overland explorers.

Marco Polo was not the first European to venture eastward to Asia. The Mongol invasion of Eastern Europe had piqued, or perhaps even forced, European curiosity about the Far East; prior to Marco Polo's journeys, Pope Innocent IV and King Louis IX of France each had sent emissaries to the Mongol Empire. Marco Polo's own father, Niccolò, and uncle, Maffeo, were both successful and far-reaching traders. It was in their company that Marco made his great trek into Asia.

This journey resulted in Marco Polo living in China for 16 or 17 years. He was originally sent with letters to Kublai

The Sea Discoveries Monument in Lisbon, Portugal. Henry the Navigator (far right) leads a cavalcade of Portuguese explorers who set sail during the Age of Discovery. Jose Elias/Lusoimages/Flickr/Getty Images

Khan from the new Pope, Gregory X, and subsequently seems to have established himself in Kublai Khan's court. But what gave Marco Polo lasting significance was that his travels were chronicled in a vivid and popular manuscript known as *Il milione*. The production of this book was something of a fluke, as it resulted from Marco Polo's meeting a writer while imprisoned by a rival community of traders. The accuracy of some of the work's content is questionable. Yet in spite of this somewhat shaky background, *Il milione* was a highly important work that helped inspire subsequent waves of European adventurers.

Not all the great explorers of the age were European. Ibn Baṭṭūṭah, a Moroccan, was said to have traveled 120,000 km (75,000 miles) throughout Asia and Africa. He helped set the tone for the spirit of discovery with his personal policy, which was "never to travel any road a second time."

What Ibn Baṭṭūṭah and Marco Polo have in common is that both left behind widely read accounts of their travels. Chronicles of this kind proved to be important on many levels. They helped widen knowledge about geography at the time and have provided subsequent generations of historians with important firsthand accounts of the cultures and events these adventurers witnessed in their travels. Perhaps most important, these tales of far-off lands helped fuel the appetite for exploration, which was about to make a major move forward by turning toward the sea.

The transition to seaborne exploration was made possible by advances in shipbuilding technology. Around the 15th century, Spanish and Portuguese shipbuilders developed a 23-m (75-foot)-tall sail craft called the caravel, which was instrumental in extending the reach of seagoing European explorers. The galley ships that preceded caravels still relied on teams of rowers. The space taken up by these men left limited room for cargo and supplies, which made galley ships unsuitable for long journeys. In addition, caravels were capable of comparatively impressive speeds and also were able to sale strongly into the wind.

The Portuguese were instrumental in developing the caravel. Portugal itself was ideally positioned geographically to pioneer exploration of the western coast of Africa by sea. Its primary reason for doing so was to establish trading relationships, although its explorers also were able to make the first colonial claims on African territory in the 15th century. A succession of Portuguese explorers steadily made their way down the west coast of Africa, with the ultimate goal of finding a route that would take them around the continent and then on to Asia.

Bartolomeu Dias was the first explorer to round the southern tip of Africa, in 1488, though he was not able to continue on to Asia. Dias originally named the southern tip of the continent the Cape of Storms, though King John II of Portugal later renamed it the Cape of Good Hope. The name given by Dias may have been more apt, however, as he was lost at sea near the cape on a later expedition. Dias's misfortune gave Vasco da Gama the opportunity to be the first to sail around the Cape of Good Hope and make it to Asia, which he did on three successful expeditions to India, beginning in 1497. His journeys helped firmly establish trade routes to the east by sea.

Explorers were also beginning to venture westward across the Atlantic, led by a native of Genoa sailing under a Spanish flag, Christopher Columbus. By the time Columbus had started soliciting financial support for his first journey across the Atlantic, he was already an established explorer and trader who had sailed as far as Ireland and Iceland to the north and along the West African coast to the south. These experiences gave Columbus invaluable knowledge concerning Atlantic sailing conditions.

As early as 1484, he was seeking backers for a voyage across the ocean, with the aim of reaching Asia via a westward route. Rebuffed by King John II of Portugal, he turned his attention to the Spanish monarchs King Ferdinand and Queen Isabella. After several years, and at least two rejections, they finally agreed to fund his expedition. Their reasons for doing so were complex; several of the aforementioned themes that fueled Renaissance exploration in general were clearly at work. Religious conflicts with Islamic nations, political maneuvering against Portugal, and the search for valuable gold and spices all played a role in the monarchs' decision. In fact, Ferdinand and Isabella were compelled by even more practical matters to consider Columbus's proposal. Islamic rulers had blocked land routes to Asia, and the Portuguese were dominating the exploration of sea routes around the African continent. Therefore, the idea of finding a back way into Asia, by sailing around the globe, was seen as being important to Spain's wealth and security.

The fact that he expected a clear path to Asia helps explains some of Columbus's faulty assumptions upon finally reaching land. Stopping first in the Bahamas, then Cuba, and ultimately on the island of Hispaniola, Columbus decided that Cuba must be the mainland of China. In any case, he returned to Spain with enough gold to justify the expedition.

While Columbus's trans-Atlantic journey is now popularly remembered as a triumph, even his brief initial visit to the New World foreshadowed some of the negative aspects of European exploration. To bring back treasure to Spain, Columbus and his men had looted native wealth and taken human captives. When he returned to Hispaniola with more than 1,000 men, religious conversion of the natives and settlement of the land were clear goals. The colonization of the New World had begun.

In total, Columbus ultimately made four voyages to the New World. Throughout his journeys he continued to insist that he had discovered the westward course to Asia, rather than an entirely new (to the European mind) land mass. This type of mistake was not unique. For example, at around the time of Columbus's later voyages, Pedro Alvares Cabral of Portugal accidentally discovered Brazil while trying to find a more hospitable route around the Cape of Good Hope. Before long, though, explorers would acknowledge their errors, complete with a greater comprehension of the importance of their discoveries. Piece-by-piece, they were filling in the puzzle that would become the map of the world as it is known today.

Each of these advances led the way for subsequent westward explorers, sailing on behalf of various western European nations. The story of one of these explorers, Amerigo Vespucci, again demonstrates the importance that chronicling one's discoveries could have. A written account of one of Vespucci's journeys across the Atlantic helped establish the notion that the lands being discovered were an entirely new continent, rather than part of Asia. This is how the name "America" came to be derived from Vespucci's first name.

Another of the westward explorers was Ferdinand Magellan. A native of Portugal, Magellan had sailed on behalf of that country for several years; a falling out with the Portuguese monarch led him to transfer his allegiance to Spain. Indeed, it is the rivalry between Portugal and Spain that led Magellan to propose circumnavigating the globe on Spain's behalf. The 1494 Treaty of Tordesillas had essentially drawn a north-to-south line in the Atlantic Ocean, designating subsequent discoveries east of that line to Portugal and discoveries west of it to Spain. With an eye toward the wealth to be had in the Moluccas, or the Spice Islands, of far-eastern Asia, Magellan reasoned that reaching those islands by sailing westward around the globe would establish them as falling west of the line, rather than east of it. Thus, he could claim them for Spain. Though Magellan was killed while attempting this journey, one of his ships did eventually complete the circumnavigation, in 1521.

Magellan's journey shows once again how political and commercial aims helped fuel Renaissance exploration. As Spain and Portugal jockeyed for advantage, members of their royal houses frequently played a role in backing voyages of discovery. For example, Prince Henry of Portugal earned the sobriquet Henry the Navigator, even though he financed rather than participated in voyages of exploration during the 15th century. Henry's interest in geography was enhanced when an older brother had an account of Marco Polo's journeys translated for him. Yet Henry's motives in financing exploration of the west coast of Africa and the islands just offshore seem primarily to have been based on commercial opportunities.

Later in the 1400s, King John II of Portugal revived Henry's tradition of supporting exploration by sea. King John funded expeditions further and further southward, down the west coast of Africa, leading to the discovery of the Cape of Good Hope by Bartolomeu Dias. By financing Columbus's 1492 journey, Spain's King Ferdinand and Queen Isabella laid the groundwork for their country to become a power in the New World.

For all the practical motives behind Renaissance exploration, the desire for adventure and a thirst for discovery still played a major role. Only such varied motivations could have been sufficient to drive the advances in geographic knowledge and navigational technology that started the evolution toward today's global society. The story behind these discoveries plays out in the pages ahead.

CHAPTER 1

THE AGE OF DISCOVERY

In the 100 years from the mid-15th to the mid-16th century, the minds of Europeans of all ranks, from kings and commoners to scholars and seamen, were filled with the dream of finding new routes by sea to Cathay, the name by which China had been known to Europe since the first overland trade was established in the Middle Ages. A combination of circumstances stimulated pursuit of these new routes. Toward the end of the 14th century, the vast empire of the Mongols was breaking up, and Western merchants could no longer be assured of safe passage along the old land routes that had long been followed across Central Asia. Compounding this problem, the growing power of the Ottoman Turks, who were hostile to Christians, blocked access from the Mediterranean to the ancient sea routes that started from the Red Sea or the Arabian Peninsula and led to the East. All roads east seemed to be closed.

The lure of Cathay had been felt in Europe since ancient times. During the reign of the Roman emperor Hadrian in the 1st century BCE, Western traders had reached Siam (now Thailand), Cambodia, Sumatra, and Java; a few also seem to have penetrated northward to the coast of China. In 161 CE, according to Chinese records, an "embassy" came from the Roman emperor

World map by J.M. Contarini, 1506, depicting the expanding horizons becoming known to European geographers in the Age of Discovery. Courtesy of the trustees of the British Museum; photograph, J.R. Freeman & Co. Ltd.

Marcus Aurelius to the emperor Huan-ti, bearing goods that Huan-ti gratefully received as "tribute." As the 2nd century CE passed and Roman power declined, trade with the eastern seas did not cease but was gradually taken over by Ethiopians, Parthians, and Arabs. The Arabs, most successful of all, dominated eastern sea routes from the 3rd to the 15th century. In the tales of derring-do of Sindbad the Sailor (a hero of the collection of Arabian tales called *The Thousand and One Nights*), there may be found, behind the fiction, the knowledge gathered by these adventurous Arab sailors and traders,

PTOLEMY'S MAPS

Claudius Ptolemaus, or Ptolemy, a Greek who flourished in Alexandria, Egypt, during the 2nd century CE, is known to history mainly as an astronomer and mathematician, but his fame as a geographer is hardly less great. His monumental work, the *Geōgraphikē hyphēgēsis* (*Guide to Geography*), was produced in eight volumes. The first volume discussed basic principles and dealt with map projection and globe construction. The next six volumes carried a list of the names of some 8,000 places and their approximate latitudes and longitudes. Except for a few that were made by observations, the greater number of these locations were determined from older maps, with approximations of distances and directions taken from travelers. The eighth volume was a most important contribution, containing instructions for preparing maps of the world and discussions on mathematical geography and other fundamental principles of cartography. Ptolemy's book thus provided all the information and techniques required to draw maps of the portion of the world that was known to his contemporaries.

By his own admission, Ptolemy did not attempt to collect and sift all the geographical data on which his maps were based. Instead, he based them on the maps and writings of Marinus of Tyre (*c.* 100 CE), only selectively introducing more current information, chiefly concerning the Asian and African coasts of the Indian Ocean. Nothing would be known about Marinus today if Ptolemy had not preserved the substance of his cartographical work.

Ptolemy's most important geographical innovation was to record longitudes and latitudes in degrees for roughly 8,000 locations on his world map, making it possible to make an exact duplicate of his map. Hence, residents of the 21st century can possess a clear and detailed image of the inhabited world as it was known to a resident of the Roman Empire at its height—a world that extended from the Shetland Islands in the north to the sources of the Nile in the south, from the Canary Islands in the west to China and Southeast Asia in the east. Ptolemy's map is seriously distorted in size and orientation compared to modern maps, but this is only a reflection of the incomplete and inaccurate descriptions of road systems and trade routes at his disposal.

Ptolemy's geographical work was almost unknown in Europe until about 1300, when Byzantine scholars began producing many manuscript copies, several of them illustrated with expert reconstructions of Ptolemy's maps. The Italian Jacopo d'Angelo translated the work into Latin in 1406. The numerous Latin manuscripts and early print editions of Ptolemy's *Guide to Geography*, most of them accompanied by maps, attest to the profound impression this work made upon its rediscovery by Renaissance humanists.

supplying detail to fill in the outline of the geography of the Indian Ocean.

By the 15th century, however, new maritime nations on the Atlantic shores of Europe such as Spain, Portugal, and England were growing in economic and military power, and they were now ready to seek overseas trade and adventure. Their image of the world was flawed, shaped by maps created by the great mathematician and astronomer Ptolemy, who had flourished in Alexandria, Egypt, more than 1,000 years before. By Ptolemy's reckoning, the Mediterranean was broader than it really was, and Europe and Asia extended over half the globe, far more than their true extent. In addition, Ptolemy calculated that the peninsula of "Colmorgo," the Malay Peninsula, swept southwestward to join the eastern coast of Africa, so that in effect the vast Indian Ocean was an enclosed inland sea.

Nevertheless, the maps provided enough information to give ambitious explorers a chance of success, and in one short century the European Age of Discovery found new routes to the East. In the process, the navigators found what to them was an entirely New World.

THE OVERLAND ROUTE TO CATHAY

The prelude to the Age of Discovery is to be found not in Arab explorations of the Indian Ocean but, rather, in the land journeys of Italian missionaries and merchants during the 13th century that linked the Mediterranean coasts to the China Sea. Cosmas Indicopleustes, an Alexandrian geographer writing in the 6th century, knew that Tzinitza (China) could be reached by sailing eastward, but he added: "One who comes by the overland route from Tzinitza to Persia makes a very short cut." Goods had certainly passed this way since Roman times, but they usually changed hands at many a mart, for disorganized and often warring tribes lived along the routes.

EUROPEANS IN THE COURT OF THE GREAT KHAN

In the 13th century, however, the political geography changed. In 1206 a Mongol chief assumed the title of Genghis Khan and, after campaigns in China that gave him control there, turned his conquering armies westward. He and his successors built up an enormous empire until, in the late 13th century, one of them, Kublai Khan, reigned supreme from the Black Sea to the Yellow Sea. Europeans of perspicacity saw the opportunities that friendship with the Mongol power might bring. If Christian Europe could only convert the Mongols, this would at one and the same time heavily tip the scales against Muslim power and in favour of Christian power, and it also would give political protection to Christian merchants along the silk routes to the legendary sources of wealth in China.

With these opportunities in mind, Pope Innocent IV sent friars to "diligently search out all things that concerned the state of the Tartars" and to exhort them "to give over their bloody slaughter of mankind and to receive the Christian faith." Among others, Giovanni Da Pian Del Carpini in 1245 and Willem Van Ruysbroeck in 1253 went forth to follow these instructions. Traveling the great caravan routes from southern Russia, north of the Caspian and Aral seas and north of the Tien Shan (Tien Mountains), both Carpini and Ruysbroeck eventually reached the court of the Mongol emperor at Karakorum. Carpini returned confident that the emperor was about to become a Christian. Ruysbroeck told of the city in Cathay "having walls of silver and towers of gold"; he had not seen it but had been "credibly informed" of it.

THE POLOS OF VENICE

The greatest of the 13th-century travelers in Asia were the Polos, wealthy merchants of Venice. In 1260 the brothers Niccolò and Maffeo Polo set out on a trading expedition to the Crimea. After two years they were ready to return to Venice, but, finding the way home blocked by war, they traveled eastward to Bukhara (now in Uzbekistan in Central Asia), where they spent another three years. The Polos then accepted an invitation to accompany a party of Tatar envoys returning to the court of Kublai Khan at Cambaluc, near Peking (Beijing). The khan received them well, provided them with a gold tablet as a safe-conduct back to Europe, and gave them a letter begging the pope

Illustration from a manuscript detailing the journey of Marco, Niccolò, and Maffei Polo setting out from Venice, bound for the court of Kublai Khan. Universal Images Group/Getty Images

to send "some hundred wise men, learned in the law of Christ and conversant with the seven arts to preach to his people."

The Polos arrived home, "having toiled three years on the way," to find that Pope Clement IV was dead. Two years later they set off again, traveling without the wise men but taking with them Niccolò's son, Marco Polo, then a youth of 17. (Marco kept detailed notes of all he saw and, late in life when a captive of the Genoese, dictated to a fellow prisoner a book containing an account of his travels and adventures.) This time the Polos took a different route: starting from the port of Hormuz on the Persian Gulf, they crossed Persia to the Pamirs and then followed a caravan route along the southern edge of the Tarim Basin and Gobi Desert to Cambaluc.

Information about the route is interesting, but the great contribution of Marco Polo to the geographical knowledge of the West lay in his vivid descriptions of the East. He had tremendous opportunities to see China and appreciate its life, for he was taken into the service of the khan and sent as an administrator to great cities, busy ports, and remote provinces, with instructions to write full reports. In his book he described how, upon every main highroad, at a distance apart of 40 to 50 km (25 or 30 miles), there were stations, with houses of accommodation for travelers, with 400 good horses kept in constant readiness at each station. He also reported that, along the roads, the great khan had caused trees to be planted, both to provide shade in summer and to mark the route in winter when the ground was covered with snow.

Marco Polo lived and worked in western China, visiting the provinces of Shensi (Shaanxi), Szechwan (Sichuan), and Yunnan, as well as the borders of Burma (now Myanmar). He frequently visited "the noble and magnificent city of Quinsay [Hangzhou], a name that signifies the Celestial City and which it merits from its pre-eminence to all others in the world in point of grandeur and beauty." Cipango (Japan) he did not visit, but he heard about it from merchants and sailors: "It is situated at a distance of 1,500 miles from the mainland....They have gold in the greatest abundance, its sources being inexhaustible." The most detailed descriptions and the greatest superlatives were reserved for Cambaluc, capital of Cathay, whose splendours were beyond compare; to this city, he said,

> *everything that is most rare and valuable in all parts*
> *of the world finds its way: ...for not fewer than 1,000*
> *carriages and pack-horses loaded with raw silk make*
> *their daily entry; and gold tissues and silks of various*
> *kinds are manufactured to an immense extent.*

No wonder that, when Europe learned of these things, it became enthralled. After 17 years, the Venetians were permitted to depart; they returned to Europe by sea. After visiting Java they sailed through the Strait of Malacca (proving the error of Ptolemy) and, landing at Hormuz, they traveled cross-country to Armenia, and so home to Venice, which they reached in 1295.

IN THE FOOTSTEPS OF THE POLOS

A few travelers followed the Polos. Giovanni da Montecorvino, a Franciscan friar from Italy, became archbishop of Beijing and lived in China from 1294 to 1328. Friar Oderic of Pordenone, an Italian monk, became a missionary, journeying throughout the greater part of Asia between 1316 and 1330. He reached Beijing by way of India and Malaya, then traveled by sea to Canton (Guangzhou); he returned to Europe by way of Central Asia, visiting Tibet in 1325—the first European to do so. Friar Oderic's account of his journeys had considerable influence in his day: it was from it that the spurious traveler, the English writer Sir John Mandeville, quarried most of his stories.

Ibn Baṭṭūṭah, an Arab of Tangier (now in Morocco), journeyed farther perhaps than any other medieval traveler. In 1325 he set out to make the traditional Muslim pilgrimage to Mecca, and in some 30 years he visited the greater part of the Old World, covering, it has been said,

Over the course of 30 years, the Moroccan explorer Ibn Baṭṭūṭah (right, shown in Egypt) visited sites throughout most of the world known to the 12th century. Universal Images Group/Getty Images

more than 120,000 km (75,000 miles). He was the first to explore much of Arabia; he traveled extensively in India; he reached Java and Southeast Asia. Then toward the end of his life he returned to the west, where, after visiting Spain, he explored western Sudan "to the northernmost province of the Negroes." He reached the Niger, which he called the Nile, and was astonished by the huge hippopotamuses "taking them to be elephants." When he finally returned to Fès in Morocco he "kissed the hand of the Commander of the Faithful the Sultan...and settled down under the wing of his bounty."

Ibn Baṭṭūṭah wrote a vivid and perspicacious account of his travels, but his book did not become known to Christian Europe for centuries. It was Marco Polo's book that was the most popular of all. Some 138 manuscripts of it survive: it was translated before 1500 into Latin, German, and Spanish, and the first English translation was published in 1577. For centuries Europe's maps of the Far East were based on the information provided by Marco Polo. Even as late as 1533 Johannes Schöner, the German maker of globes, wrote:

> *Behind the Sinae and the Ceres [legendary cities of Central Asia]...many countries were discovered by one Marco Polo...and the sea coasts of these countries have now recently again been explored by Columbus and Amerigo Vespucci in navigating the Indian Ocean.*

Columbus possessed and annotated a copy of the Latin edition (1483–85) of Marco Polo's book, and in his journal he identified many of his own discoveries with places that Marco Polo describes.

Thus, with Ptolemy in one hand and Marco Polo in the other, the European explorers of the Age of Discovery set forth to try to reach Cathay and Cipango by new ways.

Ptolemy promised that the way was short; Marco Polo promised that the reward was great.

THE SEA ROUTE EAST BY SOUTH TO CATHAY

Henry the Navigator, prince of Portugal, initiated the first great enterprise of the Age of Discovery—the search for a sea route east by south to Cathay. His motives were mixed. He was curious about the world; he was interested in new navigational aids and better ship design and was eager to test them; he was also a crusader and hoped that, by sailing south and then east along the coast of Africa, Arab power in North Africa could be attacked from the rear. The promotion of profitable trade was yet another motive; he aimed to divert the trade in gold and ivory from Guinea (West Africa) away from its routes across the Sahara to the Moors of Barbary (North Africa) and instead channel it via the sea route to Portugal.

ROUNDING THE CAPE OF GOOD HOPE

Expedition after expedition was sent forth throughout the 15th century to explore the coast of Africa. In 1445 the Portuguese navigator Dinís Dias reached the mouth of the Sénégal River (now forming part of the border between Mauritania and Senegal), which "men say comes from the Nile, being one of the most glorious rivers of Earth, flowing from the Garden of Eden and the earthly paradise." Once the desert coast had been passed, the sailors pushed on: in 1455 and 1456 Alvise Ca' da Mosto made voyages to Gambia and the Cape Verde Islands. Prince Henry died in 1460 after a career that had brought the colonization of the Madeira Islands and the Azores and the traversal of the African coast to Sierra Leone. Henry's captain, Diogo

Cão, discovered the Congo River in 1482. All seemed promising; trade was good with the riverine peoples, and the coast was trending hopefully eastward. Then the disappointing fact was realized: the head of a great gulf (the Gulf of Guinea) had been reached, and, beyond, the coast seemed to stretch endlessly southward. Yet, when Columbus sought backing for his plan to sail westward across the Atlantic to the Indies, he was refused—"seeing that King John II [of Portugal] ordered the coast of Africa to be explored with the intention of going by that route to India."

King John II sought to establish two routes: the first, a land and sea route through Egypt and Ethiopia to the Red Sea and the Indian Ocean and, the second, a sea route around the southern shores of Africa, the latter an act of faith, since Ptolemy's map showed a landlocked Indian Ocean. In 1487, a Portuguese emissary, Pêro da Covilhã, successfully followed the first route; but, on returning to Cairo, he reported that, in order to travel to India, the Portuguese "could navigate by their coasts and the seas of Guinea." In the same year, another Portuguese navigator, Bartolomeu Dias, found encouraging evidence that this was so. In 1487 he rounded the Cape of Storms in such bad weather that he did not see it, but he satisfied himself that the coast was now trending northeastward; before turning back, he reached the Great Fish River, in what is now South Africa. On the return voyage, he sighted the Cape and set up a pillar upon it to mark its discovery.

AROUND AFRICA TO MALAYSIA

The seaway was now open, but eight years were to elapse before it was exploited. In 1492 Columbus had apparently reached the East by a much easier route. By the end of the decade, however, doubts of the validity of Columbus's claim were current. Interest was therefore renewed in establishing the sea route south by east to the known riches of India. In 1497 a Portuguese captain, Vasco da Gama, sailed in command of a fleet under instructions to reach Calicut (Kozhikode), on India's west coast. This he did after a magnificent voyage around the Cape of Storms (which he renamed the Cape of Good Hope) and along the unknown coast of East Africa.

Yet another Portuguese fleet set out in 1500, this one being under the command of Pedro Álvares Cabral; on the advice of da Gama, Cabral steered southwestward to avoid the calms of the Guinea coast; thus, en route for Calicut, Brazil was discovered. Soon trading depots, known as factories, were built along the African coast, at the strategic entrances to the Red Sea and the

Elmina Castle, also known as the Castle of St. George, standing along the coast of Ghana, West Africa. The castle was once a European trading post for gold and slaves. Ariadne Van Zandbergen/Lonely Planet Images/Getty Images

Persian Gulf, and along the shores of the Indian peninsula. In 1511 the Portuguese established a base at Malacca
(now Melaka, Malaysia), commanding the straits into
the China Sea; in 1511 and 1512, the Moluccas, or Spice
Islands, and Java were reached; in 1557 the trading port
of Macau was founded at the mouth of the Canton River.
Europe had arrived in the East.

Some idea of the knowledge that these trading
explorers brought to the common store may be gained
by a study of contemporary maps. The map of the
German Henricus Martellus, published in 1492, shows
the shores of North Africa and of the Gulf of Guinea
more or less correctly and was probably taken from
numerous seamen's charts. The delineation of the west
coast of southern Africa from the Guinea Gulf to the
Cape suggests a knowledge of the charts of the expedition of Bartolomeu Dias. The coastlines of the Indian
Ocean are largely Ptolemaic with two exceptions: first,
the Indian Ocean is no longer landlocked; and second,
the Malay Peninsula is shown twice—once according to Ptolemy and once again, presumably, according
to Marco Polo. The 1506 map of Giovanni Matteo
Contarini shows further advances; the shape of Africa
is generally accurate, and there is new knowledge of
the Indian Ocean, although it is curiously treated.
Peninsular India (on which Cananor and Calicut are
named) is shown; although too small, it is, however,
recognizable. There is even an indication to the east
of it of the Bay of Bengal, with a great river running
into it. Eastward of this is Ptolemy's India, with the
huge island of Taprobane—a muddled representation
of the Indian peninsula and Ceylon (now Sri Lanka).
East again, as on the map of Henricus Martellus, the
Malay Peninsula appears twice. Ptolemy's bonds were
hard to break.

THE SEA ROUTE WEST TO CATHAY

It is not known when the idea originated of sailing west-ward in order to reach Cathay. Many sailors set forth searching for islands in the west; and it was a common-place among scientists that the east could be reached by sailing west, but to believe this a practicable voyage was an entirely different matter. Christopher Columbus, a Genoese who had settled in Lisbon about 1476, took it upon himself to prove it.

CHRISTOPHER COLUMBUS

Columbus argued that Cipango lay a mere 2,500 nautical miles (4,600 km) west of the Canary Islands in the eastern Atlantic. He took 45 (83 km) instead of 60 (111 km) nauti-cal miles as the value of a degree; he accepted Ptolemy's exaggerated west–east extent of Asia and then added to it the lands described by Marco Polo, thus reducing the true distance between the Canaries and Cipango by about one-third. He could not convince the Portuguese scientists or the merchants of Lisbon that his idea was worth backing; but eventually he obtained the support of King Ferdinand and Queen Isabella of Spain. The sovereigns probably argued that the cost of equipping the expedition would not be very great. The loss, if it failed, could be borne; the gain, should it succeed, was incalculable—indeed, it might divert to Spain all the wealth of Asia.

On Aug. 3, 1492, Columbus sailed from Palos, Spain, with three small ships manned by Spaniards. From the Canaries he sailed westward, for, on the evidence of the globes and maps in which he had faith, Japan was on the same lati-tude. If Japan should be missed, Columbus thought that the route adopted would land him, only a little further on, on the coast of China itself. Fair winds favoured him, the sea was calm, and, on October 12, landfall was made on the Bahama island of Guanahaní, which he renamed San Salvador (also called Watling Island, though Samana Cay and other islands have been identified as Guanahaní). With the help of the local Indians, the ships reached Cuba and then Haiti. Although there was no sign of the wealth of the lands of Kublai Khan, Columbus nevertheless seemed convinced that he had reached China, since, according to his reckoning, he was beyond Japan. A second voyage in 1493 and 1494, searching fruitlessly for the court of Kublai Khan, further explored the islands of "the Indies." Doubts seem to have arisen among the would-be colonists as to the identity of the islands since Columbus demanded that all take an oath that Cuba was the southeast promontory of Asia—the Golden Chersonese. On his third voyage, in 1498, Columbus sighted Trinidad, entered the Gulf of Paria, on the coast of what is now Venezuela, and annexed for Spain "a very great continent...until today unknown." On a fourth voyage, from 1502 to 1504, he explored the coast of Central America from Honduras to Darien on the Isthmus of Panama, seeking a navigable passage to the west. What passage he had in mind is obscure; if at this point he still believed he had reached Asia, it is conceivable that he sought a way through Ptolemy's Golden Chersonese into the Indian Ocean.

Columbus's tenacity, courage, and skill in navigation make him stand out among the few explorers who have changed substantially ideas about the world. At the time, however, his efforts must have seemed ill-rewarded: he found no emperor's court rich in spices, silks, gold, or precious stones but had to contend with mutinous sailors, dissident colonists, and disappointed sovereigns. He died at Valladolid in 1506. Did he believe to the end that he indeed had reached Cathay, or did he, however dimly, perceive that he had found a New World?

OTHER EXPLORATIONS

Whatever Columbus thought, it was clear to others that there was much to be investigated, and probably much to be gained, by exploration westward. Not only in Lisbon and Cádiz but also in other Atlantic ports, groups of men congregated in hopes of joining in the search. In England, Bristol, with its western outlook and Icelandic trade, was the port best placed to nurture adventurous seamen. In the latter part of the 15th century, Giovanni Caboto, with his wife and three sons, came from Genoa or Venice to Bristol, where he became known as John Cabot. His project to sail west gained support, and with one small ship, the *Matthew*, he set out in May 1497, taking a course due west from Dursey Head, Ireland. His landfall on the other side of the ocean was probably on the northern peninsula of what is now known as Newfoundland. From there, Cabot explored southward, perhaps encouraged to do so, even if seeking a westward passage, by ice in the Strait of Belle Isle. Little is known of John Cabot's first voyage, and almost nothing of his second, in 1498, from which he did not return, but his voyages in high latitudes represented almost as great a navigational feat as those of Columbus.

The coasts between the landfalls of Columbus and of John Cabot were charted in the first quarter of the 16th century by Italian, French, Spanish, and Portuguese sailors. Sebastian Cabot, son of John, gained a great reputation as a navigator and promoter of Atlantic exploration, but whether this was based primarily on his own experience or on the achievements of his father is uncertain. In 1499 Amerigo Vespucci, an Italian merchant living in Sevilla (Seville), together with the Spanish explorer Alonso de Ojeda, explored the north coast of South America from Suriname to the Golfo de Venezuela. His lively and embellished description of these lands became popular, and

Artist's depiction of John Cabot (standing on the bow) sailing off the coast of Newfoundland during the first of only two voyages the British explorer is known to have taken. Stock Montage/Archive Photos/Getty Images

German cartographer Martin Waldseemüller, on his map of 1507, gave the name America to the southern part of the continent.

The 1506 map of Contarini represented a brave attempt to collate the mass of new information, true and false, that accrued from these western voyages. The land explored by Columbus on his third voyage and by Vespucci and de Ojeda in 1499 is shown at the bottom left of the map as a promontory of a great northern bulge of a continent extending far to the south. The northeast coast of Asia at the top left is pulled out into a great peninsula on which is shown a big river and some mountains representing Contarini's concept of Newfoundland and the lands found by the Cabots and others. In the wide sea that separates these northern lands from South America, the West Indies are shown. Halfway between the Indies and the coast of Asia, Japan is drawn. A legend placed between Japan and China reveals the state of opinion among at least some contemporary geographers; it presumably refers to the fourth voyage of Columbus in 1502 and may be an addition to the map. It runs:

> *Christopher Columbus, Viceroy of Spain, sailing westwards, reached the Spanish islands after many hardships and dangers. Weighing anchor thence he sailed to the province called Ciambra [a province which then adjoined Cochinchina].*

MAGELLAN'S VOYAGE AROUND THE WORLD

Others did not agree with Contarini's interpretation. To more and more people it was becoming plain that a New World had been found, although for a long time there was little inclination to explore it but instead a great determination to find a way past it to the wealth of Asia. The voyage of the Portuguese navigator Ferdinand Magellan, from 1519 to 1521, dispelled two long-cherished illusions: first, that there was an easy way through the barrier and, second, that, once the barrier was passed, Cathay was near at hand.

Ferdinand Magellan had served in the East Indies as a young man. Familiar with the long sea route to Asia eastward from Europe via the Cape of Good Hope, he was convinced that there must be an easier sea route westward. His plan was in accord with Spanish hopes; five Spanish ships were fitted out in Sevilla, and in August 1519 they sailed under his command first to the Cape Verde Islands and thence to Brazil. Standing offshore, they then sailed southward along the east coast of South America; the estuary of the Río de la Plata was explored in the vain hope that it might prove to be a strait leading to the Pacific. Magellan's ships then sailed south along the coast of Patagonia. The Gulf of St. George, and doubtless many more small embayments, raised hopes that a strait had been found, only to dash them; at last at Port Julian, at 49°15' S, winter quarters were established.

In September 1520 a southward course was set once more, until, finally, on October 21, Magellan found a strait leading westward. It proved to be an extremely difficult one: it was long, deep, tortuous, rock-walled, and bedevilled by icy squalls and dense fogs. It was a miracle that three of the five ships got through its 525-km (325-mile) length. After 38 days, they sailed out into the open ocean. Once away from land, the ocean seemed calm enough; Magellan consequently named it the Pacific. The Pacific, however, proved to be of vast extent, and for 14 weeks the little ships sailed on a northwesterly course without encountering land. Short of food and water, the sailors ate sawdust mixed with ship's biscuits and chewed the leather parts of their gear to keep themselves alive. At last, on March 6, 1521, exhausted and scurvy-ridden, they landed at the island of Guam. Ten days later they reached the Philippines, where Magellan was killed in a local quarrel. The survivors, in two ships, sailed on to the Moluccas; thus, sailing westward, they arrived at last in territory already known to the Portuguese sailing eastward. One ship attempted, but failed, to return across the Pacific. The remaining ship, the *Vittoria*, laden with spices, under the command of the Spanish navigator Juan Sebastián del Cano, sailed alone across the Indian Ocean, rounded the Cape of Good Hope, and arrived at Sevilla on Sept. 9, 1522. It was carrying four Indians and only 18 survivors of the 239 Europeans who had set sail with the expedition three years earlier. Cano, not having allowed for the fact that his circumnavigation had caused him to lose a day, was greatly puzzled to find that his carefully kept log was one day out; he was, however, delighted to discover that the cargo that he had brought back more than paid for the expenses of the voyage.

It is fitting to consider this first circumnavigation as marking the close of the Age of Discovery. Magellan and his men had demonstrated that Columbus had discovered a New World and not the route to China and that Columbus's "Indies"—the West Indies—were separated from the East Indies by a vast ocean.

CHAPTER 2

THE GREAT OVERLAND EXPLORERS

I n the 13th and 14th centuries, a handful of determined men made the long and perilous journey across western and central Asia to the East. Some of them were sent as emissaries of the Christian world; these were the Franciscan friars Giovanni Da Pian Del Carpini, Willem Van Ruysbroeck, Giovanni da Montecorvino, and Odoric of Pordenone. Some of them went to make their fortune; the most famous of these were members of the Polo family of Venice. And some, such as the great Muslim savant Ibn Baṭṭūṭah, went for the sheer joy of seeing new lands.

GIOVANNI DA PIAN DEL CARPINI

(b. *c.* 1180, Pian del Carpine?, near Perugia, Umbria—d. Aug. 1, 1252, Antivari [Bar], Dalmatia?)

Giovanni Da Pian Del Carpini (English John of Plano Carpini), a Franciscan friar, was the first noteworthy European traveler in the Mongol Empire, to which he was sent on a formal mission by Pope Innocent IV. He wrote the earliest important Western work on Central Asia.

Giovanni was a contemporary and disciple of St. Francis of Assisi. By 1220 he was a member of the Franciscan order and subsequently became a leading Franciscan teacher in northern Europe; he held successively the offices of *custos*

("warden") in Saxony and of minister ("subordinate officer") in Germany and afterward in Spain (perhaps also in
Barbary and Cologne). He was in Cologne at the time of
the great Mongol invasion of eastern Europe and of the
disastrous Battle of Liegnitz (April 9, 1241).

Fear of the Mongols had not abated when four years
later Pope Innocent IV dispatched the first formal
Catholic mission to them, partly to protest against their
invasion of Christian territory and partly to gain reliable
information about their numbers and their plans; there
may also have been the hope of alliance with a power that
might be invaluable against Islam. At the head of the mission the Pope placed Giovanni, then already more than 60
years of age.

On Easter day, 1245, Giovanni set out. He was accompanied by Stephen of Bohemia, another friar, who was
subsequently to be left behind at Kiev. After seeking coun-
sel of Wenceslaus, king of Bohemia, the friars were joined
at Breslau (now Wrocław) by Benedict the Pole, another
Franciscan appointed to act as interpreter. The mission
entered the Mongol posts at Kanev and thereafter crossed
the Dnieper, the Don, and the Volga. On the Volga stood
the *ordu,* or "camp," of Batu, the supreme commander
on the western frontiers of the Mongol Empire and the
conqueror of eastern Europe. Giovanni and his companions, with their presents, had to pass between two fires
before being presented to Batu at the beginning of April
1246. Batu ordered them to proceed to the court of the
supreme khan in Mongolia, and accordingly, on Easter day,
April 8, 1246, they began the second and more formidable
part of their journey. Their bodies were tightly bandaged
to enable them to endure the excessive fatigue of their
great ride through Central Asia. Their route was across
the Ural (Yaik) River and north of the Caspian Sea and the
Aral Sea to the Syr Darya (Jaxartes) and the Muslim cities,

which then stood on its banks, then along the shores of the Dzungarian lakes and thence to the imperial camp of Sira Ordu (i.e., the "yellow pavilion") near Karakorum and the Orkhon River. They reached their destination on July 22, after a ride of about 5,000 km (3,000 miles) in just over 106 days.

On arriving at Sira Ordu, the Franciscans found that the interregnum that had followed the death of Ögödei, the supreme khan, or imperial ruler, had ended. His eldest son, Güyük (Kuyuk), had been designated to the throne; his formal election in a great *kuriltai,* or general assembly of shamans, was witnessed by the friars along with more than 3,000 envoys and deputies from all parts of the Mongol Empire. On August 24 they were present at the formal enthronement at the nearby camp of the "Golden" Ordu and were presented to the supreme khan. They were detained until November and were then dismissed with a letter for the Pope; this letter, written in Mongol, Arabic, and Latin, was little more than a brief imperious assertion of the khan's role as the scourge of God. The friars suffered greatly on their long winter journey homeward, and not until June 9, 1247, did they reach Kiev, where they were welcomed by the Slavic Christians as risen from the dead. Subsequently they delivered the khan's letter and made their report to the Pope, who was still at Lyon.

Immediately after his return, Giovanni recorded his observations in a large work variously styled in the manuscripts extant as *Historia Mongalorum quos nos Tartaros appellamus* ("History of the Mongols Whom We Call the Tartars") and *Liber Tartarorum* ("Book of the Tartars"), or *Tatarorum.* He divided his treatise into eight chapters on the country of the Mongols, their climate, customs, religion, character, history, policy and tactics, and on the best way of resisting them; in a ninth chapter he described the regions traversed. He added four name lists: of the peoples conquered by the Mongols, of those who had successfully to his time (1245–47) remained unconquered, of the Mongol princes, and of witnesses to the truth of his *Historia,* including several merchants trading in Kiev. His *Historia* discredited the many fables concerning the Mongols current in Western Christendom. Its account of Mongol customs and history is probably the best treatment of the subject by any medieval Christian writer, and only on geographical and personal detail is it inferior to one written a few years later by the papal envoy to the Mongols William of Rubruquis, or Rubrouck. Giovanni's companion, Benedict the Pole, also left a brief account of the mission, taken down from his dictation. Not long after his return, Giovanni was installed as archbishop of Antivari in Dalmatia and was sent as legate to Louis IX.

For a long time the *Historia* was only partially known through an abstract in the great compendium of Vincent of Beauvais (*Speculum historiale*), made a generation after Giovanni's own and first printed in 1473. Richard Hakluyt (1598) and Pierre Bergeron (1634) published portions of the text, but the complete work was not printed until 1839: M.A.P. d'Avezac (ed.) in *Recueil de voyages et de mémoires,* vol. 4, Geographical Society of Paris.

WILLEM VAN RUYSBROECK

(b. *c.* 1215 — d. *c.* 1295)

Willem Van Ruysbroeck (Latin Wilhelmus Rubruquis, English William of Rubrouck,) was a French Franciscan friar whose eyewitness account of the Mongol realm is generally acknowledged to be the best written by any medieval Christian traveler. A contemporary of the English scientist and philosopher Roger Bacon, he was cited frequently in the geographical section of Bacon's *Opus majus.*

Willem was probably from the village of Rubrouck, near Saint-Omer, France. In 1253 King Louis IX of France (St. Louis), who was then at Acre, Palestine, dispatched him on an informal mission to the Mongol Empire. Departing from Constantinople on May 7, 1253, he and his party reached the Crimean town of Sudak. There they secured oxen and carts for their long trek across the steppes to the encampment of Batu Khan, the Mongol ruler of the Volga River region. Following their arrival five weeks later, they were ordered to begin a journey of some 5,000 miles to the court of the Great Khan at Karakorum in central Mongolia.

The Christians set off on horseback on Sept. 16, 1253, their route taking them north of the Caspian and Aral seas to the Talas River, to the Cailac Valley, and to the great plains of Mongolia, and came upon the Great Khan's camp, which lay about 10 days' journey south of Karakorum.

Willem and his companions were received courteously and remained with the Khan until about July 10, 1254. They followed a more northerly route on their outward journey, reaching Tripoli on Aug. 15, 1255, where they found that Louis had returned to France in 1254.

Willem wrote about his Mongolian experiences for the French king. His narrative is free from legend and shows him to have been an intelligent and honest observer. Nothing is known about his later life, except that he was alive when Marco Polo returned from the East in 1295. After Bacon's copious use of the narrative, it was neglected, though five manuscripts survive. One copy was imperfectly reproduced by Richard Hakluyt in 1598 and 1599. A more recent Hakluyt Society edition is *The Journey of William of Rubruck to the Eastern Parts of the World, 1253–55 . . .* (1900), prepared by W.W. Rockhill.

MARCO POLO

(b. *c.* 1254, Venice [Italy]—d. Jan. 8, 1324, Venice)

Marco Polo was a Venetian merchant and adventurer who traveled from Europe to Asia in 1271–95, remaining in China for 17 of those years. His *Il milione* ("The Million"), known in English as *The Travels of Marco Polo*, is a classic of travel literature.

TRAVELS OF THE POLO FAMILY

Polo's way was paved by the pioneering efforts of his ancestors, especially his father, Niccolò, and his uncle, Maffeo. The family had traded with the Middle East for a long time, acquiring considerable wealth and prestige. Although it

Engraving of noted explorer Marco Polo. Hulton Archive/ Getty Images

is uncertain if the Polos were of the nobility, the matter was of little importance in Venice, a city of republican and mercantile traditions.

The family appears to have been shrewd, alert, and courageous; about 1260 they foresaw a political change in Constantinople (e.g., the overthrow of the Crusaders who had ruled since 1204 by Michael VIII Palaeologus in 1261), liquidated their property there, invested their capital in jewels, and set off for the Volga River, where Berke Khan, sovereign of the western territories in the Mongol Empire, held court at Sarai or Bulgar. The Polos apparently managed their affairs well at Berke's court, where they doubled their assets. When political events prevented their return to Venice, they traveled eastward to Bukhara (Bokhara) and ended their journey in 1265, probably at the grand khan's summer residence, Shangdu (immortalized as Xanadu by English poet Samuel Taylor Coleridge). Establishing friendly relations with the great Kublai Khan, they eventually returned to Europe as his ambassadors, carrying letters asking the pope to send Kublai 100 intelligent men "acquainted with the Seven Arts"; they also bore gifts and were asked to bring back oil from the lamp burning at the Holy Sepulchre in Jerusalem.

POLO'S JOURNEY TO ASIA

Little is known about Marco's early years except that he probably grew up in Venice. He was age 15 or 16 when his father and uncle returned to meet him and learned that the pope, Clement IV, had recently died. Niccolò and Maffeo remained in Venice anticipating the election of a new pope, but in 1271, after two years of waiting, they departed with Marco for the Mongol court. In Acre (now Akko, Israel) the papal legate, Teobaldo of Piacenza, gave them letters for the Mongol emperor. The Polos had been on the road for only a few days when they heard that their friend Teobaldo had been elected pope as Gregory X. Returning to Acre, they were given proper credentials, and two friars were assigned to accompany them, though they abandoned the Polos shortly after the expedition resumed.

From Acre the travelers proceeded to Ayas ("Laiazzo" in Marco's writings, now Yumurtalik, on the Gulf of İskenderun, also called the Gulf of Alexandretta, in southeastern Turkey). During the early part of 1272, they probably passed through Erzurum, in what is now eastern Turkey, and Tabriz, in what is now northern Iran, later crossing inhospitable deserts infested with brigands before reaching Hormuz on the Persian Gulf. There the Polos decided not to risk a sea passage to India and beyond but to proceed overland to the Mongol capital.

They next traveled through deserts of "surpassing aridity" toward the Khorasan region in what is now eastern Iran. Turning gradually to the northeast, they reached more hospitable lands; Badakhshān ("Balascian"), in Afghanistan, in particular, pleased the travelers. Marco suggests that they remained there for a year; detained, perhaps, by illness (possibly malaria) that was cured by the benign climate of the district. It is also believed that Marco visited territories to the south (other parts of Afghanistan, Kafiristan in the Hindu Kush, Chitral in what is now Pakistan, and perhaps Kashmir) during this period. It is, however, difficult to establish which districts he traversed and which he may have described from information gathered en route.

Leaving Badakhshān, the Polos proceeded toward the Pamirs, but the route they followed to cross these Central Asian highlands remains uncertain. Descending on the northeastern side of the chain, they reached Kashi ("Cascar") in what is now the Uygur Autonomous Region of Xinjiang, China. By this point the Polos were on the main Silk Road, and they probably followed along the oases to the south and east of the Takla Makan Desert—Yarkant ("Yarcan"), Hotan ("Cotan"), Che'erchen ("Ciarcian"), and Lop Nur (Lop Lake). These stepping-stones led to Shazhou ("Saciu") on the borders of China, a place now called Dunhuang.

Before reaching Shazhou, the Polos had traveled primarily among Muslim peoples, though they also encountered Nestorian Christians, Buddhists,

Marco Polo, his uncle, and his father presenting the pope's letter at the court of Kublai Khan, detail of an illuminated manuscript; in the Bodleian Library, Oxford, Eng. © Photos.com/Jupiterimages

Manichaeans, and Zoroastrians. In the vast province of Gansu (called "Tangut" by Marco), an entirely different civilization—mainly Buddhist in religion but partly Chinese in culture—prevailed. The travelers probably stopped in Suzhou ("Sukchu"; now Jiuquan) and Ganzhou ("Campiciu"; now Zhangye) before entering the Ningxia area. It is not clear whether they reached the Mongol summer capital of Shangdu ("Ciandu") directly or after a detour; in any event, sometime in 1275 (1274, according to the research of Japanese scholar Matsuo Otagi) the Polos were again at the Mongol court, presenting the sacred oil from Jerusalem and the papal letters to their patron, Kublai Khan.

SOJOURN IN CHINA

For the next 16 or 17 years the Polos lived in the emperor's dominions, which included, among other places, Cathay (now North China) and Mangi, or "Manzi" (now South China). They may have moved with the court from Shangdu, to the winter residence, Dadu, or "Taidu" (modern Beijing).

Unfortunately, because Marco's book *Il milione* is only incidentally a biography and autobiography, it is exceedingly difficult to ascertain where the Polos went and what they did during these years. Nevertheless, it is well known that many foreigners were in the employ of the state, since the Mongol rulers did not trust their Chinese subjects; so it would have been natural for the Polos to fit in most honourably and successfully with this motley society.

The extent of their success and the specific roles they filled, however, remains an open question. The elder Polos were probably employed in some technical capacity. Once and very abruptly, a glimpse in *Il milione* is obtained of them acting as military advisers during the siege of "Saianfu" (formerly Xiangyang, now Xiangfan), a city that was finally taken, according to Marco, thanks to some "great mangonels" (missile-throwing engines) built according to the Polos' specifications. The whole episode is dubious, however.

Marco was about age 20 when he reached Cathay. Although he knew little or no Chinese, he did speak some of the many languages then used in East Asia—most probably Turkish (in its Coman dialect) as spoken among the Mongols, Arabized Persian, Uighur (Uygur), and perhaps

Mongol. He was noticed very favourably by Kublai, who took great delight in hearing of strange countries and repeatedly sent him on fact-finding missions to distant parts of the empire. One such journey took Polo to Yunnan in southwestern China and perhaps as far as Tagaung in Myanmar (Burma); on another occasion he visited southeastern China, later enthusiastically describing the city of "Quinsay" (now Hangzhou) and the populous regions recently conquered by the Mongols. Apart from the missions he undertook for the emperor, Polo may have held other administrative responsibilities, including inspection of the customs duties and revenues collected from the trade in salt and other commodities. According to some versions of *Il milione*, he governed the city of Yangzhou for three years sometime between 1282 and 1287; but this assertion seems hardly credible and hinges entirely on the interpretation of one word. There is, however, ample evidence to show that Polo considered himself an adoptive son of his new country.

THE RETURN TO VENICE

Sometime around 1292 (1290 according to Otagi), a Mongol princess was to be sent to Persia to become the consort of Arghun Khan, and the Polos offered to accompany her. Marco wrote that Kublai had been unwilling to let them go but finally granted permission. They were eager to leave, in part, because Kublai was nearly 80, and his death (and the consequent change in regime) might have been dangerous for a small group of isolated foreigners. Naturally, they also longed to see their native Venice and their families again.

The princess, with some 600 courtiers and sailors, and the Polos boarded 14 ships, which left the port of Quanzhou ("Zaiton") and sailed southward. The fleet stopped briefly at Champa ("Ciamba," modern Vietnam) as well as a number of islands and the Malay Peninsula before settling for five months on the island of Sumatra ("Lesser Giaua") to avoid monsoon storms. There Polo was much impressed by the fact that the North Star appeared to have dipped below the horizon. The fleet then passed near the Nicobar Islands ("Necuveran"), touched land again in Sri Lanka, or Ceylon ("Seilan"), followed the west coast of India and the southern reaches of Persia, and finally anchored at Hormuz. The expedition then proceeded to Khorasan, handing over the princess not to Arghun, who had died, but to his son Maḥmūd Ghāzān.

The Polos eventually departed for Europe, but their movements at this point are unclear; possibly they stayed for a few months in Tabriz. Unfortunately, as soon as they left the Mongol dominions and set foot in a Christian country, at Trebizond in what is now Turkey, they were robbed of most of their hard-won earnings. After further delays, they reached Constantinople and finally Venice (1295). The story of their dramatic recognition by relatives and neighbours who had thought them long since dead is a part of Polo lore that is well known.

COMPILATION OF *IL MILIONE*

Soon after his return to Venice, Polo was taken prisoner by the Genoese—great rivals of the Venetians at sea—during a skirmish or battle in the Mediterranean. He was then imprisoned in Genoa, where he had a felicitous encounter with a prisoner from Pisa, Rustichello (or Rusticiano), a fairly well-known writer of romances and a specialist in chivalry and its lore, then a fashionable subject. Polo may have intended to write about his 25 years in Asia but possibly did not feel sufficiently comfortable in either Venetian or Franco-Italian; however, with

Rustichello at hand, the traveler began dictating his tale. The language employed was Franco-Italian—a strange composite tongue fashionable during the 13th and 14th centuries.

Polo was soon freed and returned to Venice. The remainder of his life can be reconstructed, in part, through the testimony of legal documents. He seems to have led a quiet existence, managing a not too conspicuous fortune and dying at age 70. His will set free a "Tatar slave" who may possibly have followed him from East Asia. A famous story relates how Polo was asked on his deathbed to retract the "fables" he had invented in his book; his answer was that he told barely half of what he actually saw.

NATURE AND CONTENT OF *IL MILIONE*

An instant success—"In a few months it spread throughout Italy," wrote Giovanni Battista Ramusio, the 16th-century Italian geographer—*Il milione* was apparently conceived as a vast cosmography based on firsthand experience. The book was not intended to be a collection of personal recollections, which leaves Polo's own personality some-what elusive, but *Divisament dou monde* ("Description of the World"), as it was originally titled, was to be the book to end all books on Asia. Nonetheless, details concerning travel, distances covered, and seasons are rarely stated; the panorama is observed from an impersonal distance with a powerful wide-angle lens. In *Il milione* Polo often branches off into descriptions of places probably visited not by himself but by his relatives or people he knew. Typical digressions are those on Mesopotamia, the Assassins and their castles, Samarkand, Siberia, Japan, India, Ethiopia, and Madagascar. *Il milione* is better understood not as biography but as part of the vernacular didactic literature, of which the Middle Ages offer many examples.

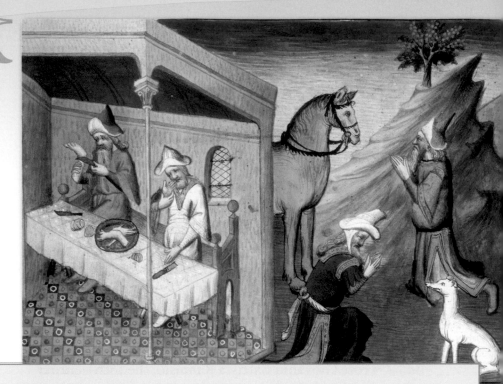

Illustration from Marco Polo's Il milone, *depicting idolatry in Sumatra.* Leemage/Universal Images Group/Getty Images

The work is marked by uncertainty and controversy, however. The origin of the popular title, *Il milione*, for example, is not quite clear. Although it most likely comes from Polo's nickname, Il milione, from his tendency to describe the millions of things he saw in the Mongol empire, it may have been related to the idea of a "tall story," or from a nickname running in the family, possibly traceable to a corruption of Aemilione ("Big Emil"). The history of the text itself is characterized by similar uncertainty. There is no authentic original manuscript, and even if there were, it would likely not represent what Polo dictated since Rustichello asserted his own personality and familiar phraseology, especially in the standardized description of battles. Polo also seems to have made emendations himself on various copies of the work during the last 20 years or so of his life.

Some editors — for instance, the friar Pipino, who made a good Latin translation of the original — found many of Polo's descriptions or interpretations impious or dangerously near to heresy and therefore heavily bowdlerized the text. Furthermore, since all this happened long before the invention of printing, professional scribes or amateurs made dozens of copies of the book, as well as free translations and adaptations — often adding to or subtracting from the text with little or no respect for authenticity. There were many unfamiliar names that rarely passed unchanged from one copy to another. Consequently, there are some 140 different manuscript versions of the text in three manuscript groups, in a dozen different languages and dialects — an immensely complex and controversial body of material representing one of the most obdurate philological problems inherited from the Middle Ages.

SUBSEQUENT REPUTATION

As a result of Polo's reticence concerning personal matters and the controversies surrounding the text, Polo's reputation has suffered dramatic ups and downs. For some scholars, novelists, filmmakers, and dramatists, he was a brilliant young courtier, a man of prodigious memory, a most conscientious observer, and a successful official at the cosmopolitan court of the Mongol rulers. For others he was a braggart, a drifter ready to believe the gossip of ports and bazaars, a man with little culture, scant imagination, and a total lack of humour. Still others argue that he never went to China at all, noting that he failed, among other things, to mention the Great Wall of China, the use of tea, and the ideographic script of the Far East, and that contemporary Chinese records show no trace of Polo. (But under what name was he known? Who would recognize the 16th- and 17th-century Italian missionary Matteo Ricci under Li Matou or the 18th-century painter Giuseppe Castiglione under Lang Shining?)

A more balanced view must take into account many factors, especially the textual problem and medieval ideas of the world. Modern scholarship and research have, however, given a new depth and scope to his work. It is generally recognized that he reported faithfully what he saw and heard, but that much of what he heard was fabulous or distorted. In any case, Polo's account opened new vistas to the European mind, and as Western horizons expanded, Polo's influence grew as well. His description of Japan set a definite goal for Christopher Columbus in his journey in 1492, while his detailed localizations of spices encouraged Western merchants to seek out these areas and break the age-old Arab trading monopoly. The wealth of new geographic information recorded by Polo was widely used in the late 15th and the 16th centuries, during the age of the great European voyages of discovery and conquest.

GIOVANNI DA MONTECORVINO

(b. 1247, Montecorvino, Sicily—d. 1328, Beijing, China)

Giovanni da Montecorvino was an Italian Franciscan missionary who founded the earliest Roman Catholic missions in India and China and became the first archbishop of Beijing.

In 1272 Montecorvino was commissioned by the Byzantine emperor Michael VIII Palaeologus as an emissary to Pope Gregory X to negotiate the reunion of Greek and Roman churches. He began his missionary work in Armenia and Persia *c.* 1280. In 1289 Pope Nicholas

IV sent him as emissary to the Il-Khan of Persia. From Tabriz, then the chief city of western Asia, Montecorvino moved down to the Madras region of India, from which he wrote (1292/93) the earliest noteworthy Western account of that region of the Indian seaboard known historically as the Coromandel Coast. In 1294 he entered Khanbaliq (Beijing). His letters of 1305 and 1306 describe the progress of the Roman mission in the Far East—including opposition by the Nestorian Christians—and allude to the Roman Catholic community he had founded in India.

In 1307 Pope Clement V named him archbishop of Beijing and patriarch of Asia. Seven bishops were sent to consecrate and assist him; only three of them survived the journey. A Franciscan tradition maintains that in 1311 Montecorvino baptized Khaishan Külüg, the third great khan (1307–11), and his mother. This event has been disputed, but he was unquestionably successful in northern and eastern China. He was apparently the only effective European proselytizer in medieval Beijing, but the results of his mission were lost in the downfall of the Mongol Empire during the 14th century.

ODORIC OF PORDENONE

(b. c. 1286, Villanova, near Pordenone, Aquileia [Italy]—d. Jan. 14, 1331, Udine)

Odoric of Pordenone was a Franciscan friar and traveler whose account of his journey to China enjoyed wide popularity and appears to have been plagiarized in the 14th-century English work *The Voyage and Travels of Sir John Mandeville, Knight*, generally known as *The Travels of Sir John Mandeville*.

After taking his vows at Udine, Odoric was sent to Asia (c. 1316–18), where he remained until 1329. Passing through Asia Minor, he visited Franciscan houses at Trabzon and

Erzurum, now in Turkey. He circled through Persia, stopping at the Franciscan house at Tabriz and continuing on to Kashan, Yazd, Persepolis, and Shīrāz before touring the Baghdad region of Mesopotamia. He then went to Hormuz (now in Iran) at the southern end of the Persian Gulf and eventually embarked for India.

After landing at Thāna, near Bombay, about 1322, Odoric visited many parts of India and possibly Ceylon. He sailed in a junk for the north coast of Sumatra, touching on Java and perhaps Borneo before reaching the south China coast. He traveled extensively in China and visited Hang-chou (Hangzhou), renowned as the greatest city in the world, whose splendour he described in detail. After three years at Beijing, he set out for home, probably by way of Tibet (including Lhasa) and northern Persia. By the time he reached Italy, he had baptized more than

Scene featuring the travels of Odoric of Pordenone, shown riding a horse outside Beijing, China. Throughout his travels Odoric, who was a friar, baptized the natives of the lands he visited. The Bridgeman Art Library/ Getty Images

20,000 persons. At Padua the story of his travels was taken down in simple Latin by another friar. Several months later Odoric died while on the way to the papal court at Avignon.

The story of his journeys seems to have made a greater impression on the laity of Udine than on Odoric's Franciscan brethren. The latter were about to bury him when the chief magistrate (*gastaldi*) of the city interfered and ordered a public funeral. Popular acclamation made Odoric an object of devotion, and the municipality erected a shrine for his body. Although his fame was widespread before the middle of the 14th century, he was not formally beatified until 1755.

IBN BAṬṬŪṬAH

(b. Feb. 24, 1304, Tangier, Morocco—d. 1368/69 or 1377, Morocco)

Abū 'Abd Allāh Muḥammad ibn 'Abd Allāh al-Lawātī al-Ṭanjī ibn Baṭṭūṭah, the greatest medieval Arab traveler, was the author of one of the most famous travel books, the *Riḥlah (Travels)*, which describes his extensive travels to almost all the Muslim countries and as far as China and Sumatra.

LIFE AND TRAVELS

Ibn Baṭṭūṭah was from a family that produced a number of Muslim judges (qāḍīs). He received the traditional juristic and literary education in his native town of Tangier. In 1325, at the age of 21, he started his travels by undertaking the pilgrimage to Mecca. At first his purpose was to fulfill this religious duty and to broaden his education by studying under famous scholars in the Near East (Egypt, Syria, and the Hejaz). That he achieved his objectives is corroborated

THE SPURIOUS TALES OF SIR JOHN MANDEVILLE

Sir John Mandeville is the purported author of a 14th-century collection of travelers' tales from around the world, *The Voyage and Travels of Sir John Mandeville, Knight*, generally known as *The Travels of Sir John Mandeville*. The tales are selections from the narratives of genuine travelers, embellished with Mandeville's additions and described as his own adventures.

The actual author of the tales remains as uncertain as the existence of the English knight Sir John Mandeville himself. The book originated in French about 1356–57 and was soon translated into many languages, an English version appearing about 1375. The narrator Mandeville identifies himself as a knight of St. Albans. Incapacitated by arthritic gout, he has undertaken to stave off boredom by writing of his travels, which began on Michaelmas Day (September 29) 1322,

Illustration from The Travels of Sir John Mandeville, *c. 1372.* © Photos.com/Jupiterimages

and from which he returned in 1356. The 14th-century chronicler Jean d'Outremeuse of Liège claimed that he knew the book's true author, a local physician named Jean de Bourgogne, and scholars afterward speculated that d'Outremeuse himself wrote the book. Modern historical research debunked the d'Outremeuse tradition but has yielded few more positive conclusions, and the actual author of the *Travels* remains unknown.

It is not certain whether the book's true author ever traveled at all, since he selected his materials almost entirely from the encyclopaedias and travel books available to him, including those by William of Boldensele and Friar Odoric of Pordenone. The author enriched these itineraries with accounts of the history, customs, religions, and legends of the regions visited, culled from his remarkably wide reading, transforming and enlivening the originals by his literary skill and genuine creative imagination. The lands that he describes include the realm of Prester John, the land of darkness, and the abode of the Ten Lost Tribes of Israel, all legendary. Although in his time "Mandeville" was famous as the greatest traveler of the Middle Ages, in the ensuing age of exploration he lost his reputation as a truthful narrator. His book, notwithstanding, has always been popular and remains extremely readable.

by long enumerations of scholars and Sufi (Islamic mystic) saints whom he met and also by a list of diplomas conferred upon him (mainly in Damascus). These studies qualified him for judicial office, whereas the claim of being a former pupil of the then-outstanding authorities in traditional Islamic sciences greatly enhanced his chances and made him thereafter a respected guest at many courts.

But this was to follow later. In Egypt, where he arrived by the land route via Tunis and Tripoli, an irresistible passion for travel was born in his soul, and he decided to visit as many parts of the world as possible, setting as a rule "never to travel any road a second time." His contemporaries traveled for practical reasons (such as trade, pilgrimage, and education), but Ibn Baṭṭūṭah did it for its own sake, for the joy of learning about new countries and new peoples. He made a living of it, benefitting at the beginning from his scholarly status and later from his increasing fame as a traveler. He enjoyed the generosity and benevolence of numerous sultans, rulers, governors, and high dignitaries in the countries he visited, thus securing an income that enabled him to continue his wanderings.

From Cairo, Ibn Baṭṭūṭah set out via Upper Egypt to the Red Sea but then returned and visited Syria, there joining a caravan for Mecca. Having finished the pilgrimage in 1326, he crossed the Arabian Desert to Iraq, southern Iran, Azerbaijan, and Baghdad. There he met the last of the Mongol khans of Iran, Abū Saʿīd (ruled 1316–36), and some lesser rulers. Baṭṭūṭah spent the years between 1327 and 1330 in Mecca and Medina leading the quiet life of a devotee, but such a long stay did not suit his temperament.

Embarking on a boat in Jiddah, he sailed with a retinue of followers down both shores of the Red Sea to Yemen, crossed it by land, and set sail again from Aden. This time he navigated along the eastern African coast, visiting the trading city-states as far as Kilwa (Tanzania). His return journey took him to southern Arabia, Oman, Hormuz, southern Persia, and across the Persian Gulf back to Mecca in 1332.

There a new, ambitious plan matured in his mind. Hearing of the sultan of Delhi, Muḥammad ibn Tughluq (ruled 1325–51), and his fabulous generosity to Muslim scholars, he decided to try his luck at his court. Forced by lack of communications to choose a more indirect route, Ibn Baṭṭūṭah turned northward, again passed Egypt and

Syria, and boarded ship for Asia Minor in Latakia. He crisscrossed this "land of the Turks" in many directions at a time when Anatolia was divided into numerous petty sultanates. Thus, his narrative provides a valuable source for the history of this country between the end of the Seljuq power and the rise of the house of Ottoman. Ibn Baṭṭūṭah was received cordially and generously by all the local rulers and heads of religious brotherhoods (ākhīs).

His journey continued across the Black Sea to the Crimea, then to the northern Caucasus and to Saray on the lower Volga, capital of the khan of the Golden Horde, Muḥammad Özbeg (ruled 1312–41). According to his narrative, he undertook an excursion from Saray to Bulgary on the upper Volga and Kama, but there are reasons to doubt his veracity on this point. On the other hand, the narrative of his visit to Constantinople in the retinue of the khan's wife, a Byzantine princess, seems to be an eyewitness record, although there are some minor chronological discrepancies. Ibn Baṭṭūṭah's description of the Byzantine capital is vivid and, in general, accurate. Although he shared the strong opinions of his fellow Muslims toward unbelievers, his account of the "second Rome" shows him as a rather tolerant man with a lively curiosity. Nevertheless, he always felt happier in the realm of Islam than in non-Muslim lands, whether Christian, Hindu, or pagan.

After his return from Constantinople through the Russian steppes, he continued his journey in the general direction of India. From Saray he traveled with a caravan to Central Asia, visiting the ancient towns of Bukhara, Samarkand, and Balkh, all of these still showing the scars left by the Mongol invasion. He took rather complicated routes through Khorāsān and Afghanistan, and, after crossing the Hindu Kush (mountains), he arrived at the frontiers of India on the Indus River on Sept. 12, 1333, by his own dating.

The accuracy of this date is doubtful, as it would have been impossible to cover such enormous distances (from Mecca) in the course of only one year. Because of this discrepancy, his subsequent dating until 1348 is highly uncertain.

At this time he was already a man of some importance and fame, with a large train of attendants and followers and also with his own harem of legal wives and concubines. India and its ruler, Muḥammad ibn Tughluq, lived up to Ibn Baṭṭūṭah's expectations of wealth and generosity, and the traveler was received with honours and gifts and later appointed grand qāḍī of Delhi, a sinecure that he held for several years.

Though he had apparently attained an easy life, it soon became clear that his new position was not without danger. Sultan Muḥammad, an extraordinary mixture of generosity and cruelty, held sway over the greater part of India with an iron hand that fell indiscriminately upon high and low, Muslim and Hindu alike. Ibn Baṭṭūṭah witnessed all the glories and setbacks of the sultan and his rule, fearing daily for his life as he saw many friends fall victim to the suspicious despot. His portrait of Muḥammad is an unusually fine piece of psychological insight and mirrors faithfully the author's mixed feelings of terror and sympathy. Notwithstanding all his precautions, Baṭṭūṭah at last fell into disgrace, and only good fortune saved his life; gaining favour again, he was appointed the Sultan's envoy to the Chinese emperor in 1342.

He left Delhi without regrets, but his journey was full of other dangers: not far away from Delhi his party was waylaid by Hindu insurgents, and the traveler barely escaped with his life. On the Malabar Coast he became involved in local wars and was finally shipwrecked near Calicut, losing all his property and the presents for the Chinese emperor. Fearing the wrath of the Sultan, Ibn Baṭṭūṭah chose to go to the Maldive Islands, where he spent nearly two years; as a qāḍī, he was soon active in politics, married into the ruling family, and apparently even aspired to become sultan.

Finding the situation too dangerous, he set out for Ceylon (Sri Lanka), where he visited the ruler as well as the famous Adam's Peak. After a new shipwreck on the Coromandel Coast, of eastern India, he took part in a war led by his brother-in-law and went again to the Maldives and then to Bengal and Assam. At this time he decided to resume his mission to China and sailed for Sumatra. There he was given a new ship by the Muslim sultan and started for China; his description of his itinerary contains some discrepancies.

He landed at the great Chinese port Zaytūn (identified as Quanzhou, near Xiamen [Amoy]) and then traveled on inland waterways as far as Beijing and back. This part of his narrative is rather brief, and the itinerary, as well as the chronology, presents many problems and difficulties, not yet surmounted, that cast shadows of doubt on his veracity.

Equally brief is his account of the return voyage via Sumatra, Malabar, and the Persian Gulf to Baghdad and Syria. In Syria he witnessed the ravages of the Black Death of 1348, visited again many towns there and in Egypt, and in the same year performed his final pilgrimage to Mecca. At last he decided to return home, sailing from Alexandria to Tunisia, then to Sardinia and Algiers, finally reaching Fès, the capital of the Marīnid sultan, Abū 'Inān, in November 1349.

But there still remained two Muslim countries not yet known to him. Shortly after his return he went to the kingdom of Granada, the last remnant of Moorish Spain, and two years later (in 1352) he set out on a journey to the western Sudan. His last journey (across the Sahara to Western Africa) was taken unwillingly at the command of the sultan. Crossing the Sahara, he spent a year in the

empire of Mali, then at the height of its power under
Mansa Sulaymān; his account represents one of the most
important sources of that period for the history of that
part of Africa.

Toward the end of 1353 Ibn Baṭṭūṭah returned to
Morocco and, at the sultan's request, dictated his reminis-
cences to a writer, Ibn Juzayy (died 1355), who embellished
the simple prose of Ibn Baṭṭūṭah with an ornate style and
fragments of poetry. After that he passes from sight. He
is reported to have held the office of qadi in a town in
Morocco before his death, details of which remain uncertain. It has been suggested that he died in 1368/69 or 1377
and was buried in his native town of Tangier.

ASSESSMENT

The claim of Ibn Baṭṭūṭah to be "the traveler of Islam" is
well founded: it is estimated that the extent of his wanderings was more than 120,000 km (75,000 miles), a figure
hardly surpassed by anyone before the age of steam. He
visited, with few exceptions (central Persia, Armenia, and
Georgia), all Muslim countries, as well as many adjacent
non-Muslim lands. While he did not discover new or
unknown lands, and his contribution to scientific geography was minimal, the documentary value of his work has
given it lasting historical and geographical significance.
He met at least 60 rulers and a much greater number of
viziers, governors, and other dignitaries; in his book he
mentioned more than 2,000 persons who were known to
him personally or whose tombs he visited. The majority of
these persons are identifiable by independent sources, and
there are surprisingly few errors in names or dates in Ibn
Baṭṭūṭah's material.

His Riḥlah, as his book is commonly known, is an
important document shedding light on many aspects of

the social, cultural, and political history of a great part of the Muslim world. A curious observer interested in the ways of life in various countries, he describes his experiences with a human approach rarely encountered in official historiography. His accounts of his travels in Asia Minor, East and West Africa, the Maldives, and India form a major source for the histories of these areas, whereas the parts dealing with the Arab and Persian Near East are valuable for their wealth of detail on various aspects of social and cultural life.

On the whole, Ibn Baṭṭūṭah is reliable; only his alleged journey to Bulgary was proved to be invented, and there are some doubts concerning the Far Eastern part of his travels. A few grave and several minor discrepancies in the chronology of his travels are due more to lapses in his memory than to intentional fabrication. A number of formerly uncertain points (such as travels in Asia Minor and the visit to Constantinople) have since been cleared away by contemporary research and the discovery of new corroborative sources.

Another interesting aspect of the Riḥlah is the gradual revealing of the character of Ibn Baṭṭūṭah himself; in the course of the narrative the reader may learn the opinions and reactions of an average middle-class Muslim of the 14th century. He was deeply rooted in orthodox Islam but, like many of his contemporaries, oscillated between the pursuit of its legislative formalism and an adherence to the mystic path and succeeded in combining both. He did not offer any profound philosophy but accepted life as it came to him, leaving to posterity a true picture of himself and his times.

CHAPTER 3

THE GREAT EASTWARD NAVIGATORS

During the 15th and 16th centuries, Portuguese navigators (or foreign navigators sailing in the service of Portugal) such as Dinís Dias, Alvise Ca' da Mosto, and Diogo Cão pushed farther down the western coast of Africa until the southernmost point of the continent was rounded by Bartolomeu Dias. Meanwhile, Pêro da Covilhã crossed the northern part of the continent by land. Finally, Vasco da Gama and Pedro Álvares Cabral sailed up the eastern coast of Africa (Cabral having first crossed the Atlantic and explored the coast of Brazil) and established the Portuguese presence in India.

DINÍS DIAS

(fl. 15th century)

Dinís Dias was a Portuguese navigator and explorer, one of the sea captains sent along the Atlantic coast of northern Africa by Prince Henry the Navigator.

As captain of a caravel in 1445, Dias sailed past the outflooding mouth of the Sénégal River, later discovering Cape Verde, the westernmost point of Africa. Dias chose the name "Green Cape" because the headland had tall trees and fragrant vegetation. Dias and his crew were repulsed by natives when they tried to land and soon returned to Portugal.

A modern-day view of Cape Verde, the area along the West African coast discovered by the Portuguese explorer Dinís Diaz. Patrice Hauser/ StockImage/Getty Images

In 1446 Prince Henry formed a fleet of caravels that were to show the Portuguese flag along the African coast and explore the river of Senegal, which the Portuguese believed was the western branch of the Nile. Dias commanded one of the vessels.

ALVISE CA' DA MOSTO

(b. 1432, Venice—d. July 18, 1488, Venice)

Alvise Ca' da Mosto (also spelled Cadamosto) was a Venetian traveler and nobleman who wrote one of the earliest known accounts of western Africa.

Accompanied by Italian explorer Antoniotto Usodimare and financed by Prince Henry the Navigator, Ca' da Mosto set sail on March 22, 1455. He visited Madeira and the Canary Islands, and coasted along Africa past the mouth of the Sénégal River. He ascended some distance up the Gambia River, but, finding the people hostile, he returned to Portugal.

Ca' da Mosto's company appears to have been the first European expedition to reach the Cape Verde Islands, two of which he explored (1456) and found uninhabited. Returning to the African shore, he sailed south from the region of the Gambia to the coast of modern Guinea-Bissau. His account of the voyage contains an impressive study of Senegambian ethnography and slavery. He is credited with creating a portolan chart—a chart of sailing directions—for the Mediterranean that was later widely used by Italian navigators.

DIOGO CÃO

(fl. 1480–86)

Diogo Cão (also spelled Cam) was a Portuguese navigator and explorer. Cão was the first European to discover the mouth of the Congo River (August 1482). There he set up a stone pillar to mark Portuguese over-lordship of the area. Sailing a short way upstream, he found that the inhabitants along the banks appeared willing to trade. He then traveled southward along the present Angola coast and erected a second pillar at Cape Santa Maria (Monte Negro, 13°26' S). Upon his return to Lisbon in 1484 he was ennobled by King John II, granted an annuity, and authorized to add two pillars to his coat of arms in memory of those he had erected. On a second voyage (1485–86) he reached Cape Cross, 21°50' S, now in Namibia.

PÊRO DA COVILHÃ

(b. *c.* 1460, Covilhã, Portugal—d. after 1526)

Pêro da Covilhã (also spelled Pedro de Covilham, or Covilhão) was an early Portuguese explorer of Africa who established relations between Portugal and Ethiopia.

As a boy, Pêro served the duke of Medina-Sidonia in Sevilla (Seville) for six or seven years, returning to Portugal with the duke's brother late in 1474 or early in 1475, when he passed into the service of King Afonso V, first as a junior squire and then as squire, serving with horse and arms. He accompanied the king when he claimed the Castilian throne and was proclaimed at Plasencia, and he was present at the Battle of Toro. He also escorted the king on a fruitless journey to France to seek aid from Louis XI. On Afonso's death, Pêro served his son John II as a squire of the royal guard and was employed as a confidential messenger to Spain. He was sent on two missions to North Africa, one, in the guise of a merchant, to seek the friendship of the ruler of Tlemcen, and the other to Fez to buy horses for Dom Manuel, later king (as Manuel I).

John II hoped to profit from the spice trade of India and to make contact with the Christian ruler of Abyssinia (Ethiopia), identified with the semimythical Prester John. Abyssinians had already visited Rome and even the Iberian Peninsula. John had sent Diogo Cão (Diogo Cam) down the west coast of Africa, and he had discovered the Congo and sailed beyond, but his belief that he had reached or was about to reach the cape proved unfounded. John then ordered Bartolomeu Dias to pursue Cão's explorations. He also decided to send travelers by land to report on the location and trade of India and Abyssinia. This move may have resulted from reports received in 1486 in Benin (a kingdom on the west coast of Africa), referring to a great ruler far to the east. Pêro was chosen for the mission to India, and Afonso de Paiva, a squire who spoke Arabic, was to seek Prester John and discover a route from Guinea to Abyssinia. The men left Portugal in May 1487 with letters of credit on Italian bankers; they reached Barcelona and sailed to Naples and Rhodes, where they assumed the guise of honey merchants and sailed to Alexandria. They became ill, and their wares were seized, but they bought other goods and went to Cairo, joining a group of North Africans traveling to Aden. There they separated, Pêro going to India, reaching Cannanore, Calicut, and Goa. He then returned to Ormuz, in Persia, sometime between October 1489 and March 1490. Meanwhile, Afonso de Paiva had reached Abyssinia. The two had proposed to meet at Cairo. Pêro arrived there about the end of 1490 or early 1491 and received news of his companion's death. Meanwhile, John II had sent two messengers to Cairo to instruct Pêro to return when the mission was completed. Pêro wrote a letter to John about his experiences and continued on to Abyssinia. One of the messengers accompanied him to Ormuz, where they separated. Pêro made his way to the Red Sea. Disguised as a Muslim, he visited Mecca and Medina. He also saw Mount Sinai, reaching Zeila in 1492 or 1493, whence he passed by caravan to Abyssinia, where he was destined to spend the rest of his life.

Pêro was received by the Abyssinian ruler, Emperor Eskender, and was well treated and made governor of a district. He was not, however, allowed to leave the country. Some years later the Abyssinian regent, Queen Helena, sent an Armenian named Matthew to Portugal. He reached Afonso de Albuquerque at Goa in 1512 and was in Portugal in 1514. It was then decided to send a Portuguese embassy to Abyssinia. The first ambassador died, and his successor, Dom Rodrigo de Lima, and his party left from India in 1517 and finally reached the emperor's camp in December 1520. They found Pêro old but robust, and he served them as guide and interpreter. When they returned in 1524, Pêro and his wife and family accompanied them for part of the way, and he sent his 23-year-old son with Dom Rodrigo to be educated in Portugal.

BARTOLOMEU DIAS

(b. *c.* 1450—d. May 29, 1500, at sea, near Cape of Good Hope)

Bartolomeu Dias (also spelled Diaz) was a Portuguese navigator and explorer who led the first European

Monument to Bartolomeu Dias erected in Cape Town, South Africa. Charged with finding the southernmost point of the African continent, Dias rounded the Cape of Good Hope in 1488. Panoramic Images/Getty Images

expedition to round the Cape of Good Hope (1488), opening the sea route to Asia via the Atlantic and Indian oceans. He is usually considered to be the greatest of the Portuguese pioneers who explored the Atlantic during the 15th century.

Almost nothing is known of Dias' early life. His supposed descent from one of Prince Henry the Navigator's pilots is unproved, and his rank was the comparatively modest one of squire of the royal household.

In 1474, King Afonso V entrusted his son, Prince John (later John II), with the supervision of Portugal's trade with Guinea and the exploration of the western coast of Africa. John sought to close the area to foreign shipping and after his accession in 1481 ordered new voyages of discovery to ascertain the southern limit of the African continent. The navigators were given stone pillars (*padrões*) to stake the claims of the Portuguese crown. Thus one of them, Diogo Cão, reached the Congo and sailed down the coast of Angola to Cape Santa Maria at 13°26' S, where he planted one of John's markers. Cão was ennobled and rewarded and sailed again: this time he left a marker at 15°40' and another at Cape Cross, continuing to 22°10' S. Royal hopes that he would reach the Indian Ocean were disappointed, and nothing more is heard of Cão. John II entrusted command of a new expedition to Dias. In 1486 rumour arose of a great ruler, the Ogané, far to the east, who was identified with the legendary Christian ruler Prester John. John II then sent Pêro da Covilhã and one Afonso Paiva overland to locate India and Abyssinia and ordered Dias to find the southern limit of Africa.

Dias' fleet consisted of three ships, his own *São Cristóvão*, the *São Pantaleão* under his associate João Infante, and a supply ship under Dias' brother, whose name is variously given as Pêro or Diogo. The company included some of the leading pilots of the day, among them

Pêro de Alenquer and João de Santiago, who earlier had sailed with Cão. A 16th-century historian, João de Barros, places Dias' departure in August 1486 and says that he was away 16 months and 17 days, but since two other contemporaries, Duarte Pacheco and Christopher Columbus, put his return in December 1488, it is now usually supposed that he left in August 1487.

Dias passed Cão's marker, reaching the "Land of St. Barbara" on December 4, Walvis Bay on December 8, and the Gulf of St. Stephen (Elizabeth Bay) on December 26. After Jan. 6, 1488, he was prevented by storms from proceeding along the coast and sailed south out of sight of land for several days. When he again turned to port, no land appeared, and it was only on sailing north that he sighted land on February 3. He had thus rounded the Cape without having seen it. He called the spot Angra de São Brás (Bay of St. Blaise, whose feast day it was) or the Bay of Cowherds, from the people he found there. Dias's black companions were unable to understand these people, who fled but later returned to attack the Portuguese. The expedition went on to Angra da Roca (present-day Algoa Bay). The crew was unwilling to continue, and Dias recorded the opinions of all his officers, who were unanimously in favour of returning. They agreed to go on for a few days, reaching Rio do Infante, named after the pilot of *São Pantaleão*; this is almost certainly the present Great Fish (Groot-Vis) River.

Faced with strong currents, Dias turned back. He sighted the Cape itself in May. Barros says that he named it Cape of Storms and that John II renamed it Cape of Good Hope. Duarte Pacheco, however, attributes the present name to Dias himself, and this is likely since Pacheco joined Dias at the island of Príncipe. Little is known of the return journey, except that Dias touched at Príncipe, the Rio do Resgate (in the present Liberia), and the fortified

THE CARAVEL

Europe had made some progress in discovery before the Age of Exploration, Genoese seamen having discovered the Madeira Islands and the Azores in the 14th century. These discoveries could not be followed up immediately, however, because they had been made in galleys built for the Mediterranean and ill suited to ocean travel. In addition, the numerous rowers that they required and their lack of substantial holds left only limited room for provisions and cargo.

In the early 15th century, all-sails vessels, called caravels, largely superseded galleys for Atlantic travel. Caravels were light ships, having usually two but sometimes three masts, ordinarily equipped with triangular lateen sails but occasionally square-rigged. Apparently developed by the Portuguese for exploring the coast of Africa, the caravel's chief excellence lay

A replica of a 15th-century caravel sailing into Chicago's Navy Pier in 2000. Tim Boyle/Getty Images

in its capacity for sailing to windward. It was also capable of remarkable speed. Two of the three ships in which Christopher Columbus made his historic voyage in 1492 were caravels, the *Niña* and the *Pinta.*

The design of caravels underwent changes over the years, but a typical caravel of the late 15th century may be described as a broad-beamed vessel of 50 or 60 tons burden; some were as large as 160 tons. About 23 metres (75 feet) long, the typical caravel had two or three pole masts, lateen-rigged. Later versions added a fourth mast with square sail for running before the wind. Caravels were usually built with a double tower at the stern (the aftercastle, or sterncastle) and a single tower in the bow (the forecastle). As a type, caravels were smaller and lighter than the Spanish galleons of the 16th century. When longer voyages began, the *nao*, or carrack, proved better than the caravel; it had three masts and square rigging and was a rounder, heavier ship, more fitted to cope with ocean winds.

trading post of Mina. One of Dias's markers, at Padrão de São Gregório, was retrieved from False Island, about 30 miles short of the Great Fish River, in 1938. Another marker once stood at the western end of the Gulf of St. Christopher, since renamed Dias Point.

Nothing is known of Dias's reception by John II. Although plans are said to have been made for a voyage to India, none is known to have been attempted for nine years, perhaps pending news of Pêro da Covilhã. Dias died in 1500 after his ship was lost at sea near the Cape of Good Hope.

Dias had a son, António, and his grandson, Paulo Dias de Novais, governed Angola and became the founder of the first European city in southern Africa, São Paulo de Luanda, in 1576.

VASCO DA GAMA

(b. *c.* 1460, Sines, Portugal—d. Dec. 24, 1524, Cochin, India)

Vasco da Gama, 1er conde da Vidigueira, was a Portuguese navigator whose voyages to India (1497–99, 1502–03, 1524) opened up the sea route from western Europe to the East by way of the Cape of Good Hope.

Da Gama was the third son of Estêvão da Gama, a minor provincial nobleman who was commander of the fortress of Sines on the coast of Alentejo province in southwestern Portugal. Little is known of his early life. In 1492 King John II of Portugal sent him to the port of Setúbal, south of Lisbon, and to the Algarve, Portugal's southernmost province, to seize French ships in retaliation for French peacetime depredations against Portuguese shipping—a task that da Gama rapidly and effectively performed.

In 1495 King Manuel ascended to the throne. The balance of power between factions at the Portuguese court shifted in favour of friends and patrons of the da Gama family. Simultaneously, a neglected project was revived: to send a Portuguese fleet to India to open the sea route to Asia and to outflank the Muslims, who had hitherto enjoyed a monopoly of trade with India and other eastern states. For unknown reasons, da Gama, who had little relevant experience, was appointed to lead the expedition.

THE FIRST VOYAGE

Da Gama sailed from Lisbon on July 8, 1497, with a fleet of four vessels—two medium-sized three-masted sailing ships, each of about 120 tons, named the *São Gabriel* and the *São Rafael*; a 50-ton caravel, named the *Berrio*; and a 200-ton storeship. With da Gama's fleet went three interpreters—two Arabic speakers and one who spoke several Bantu dialects. The fleet also carried *padrões* (stone pillars) to set up as marks of discovery.

Passing the Canary Islands on July 15, the fleet reached São Tiago in the Cape Verde Islands on the 26th, remaining there until August 3. Then, to avoid the currents of the Gulf of Guinea, da Gama undertook a long detour through the South Atlantic before attempting to round the Cape of Good Hope. The fleet reached Santa Helena Bay (in modern South Africa) on November 7. Unfavourable winds and the adverse current delayed the rounding of the Cape of Good Hope until November 22. Three days later da Gama anchored in Mossel Bay, erected a *padrão* on an island, and ordered the storeship to be broken up. Sailing again on December 8, the fleet reached the coast of Natal on Christmas Day. On Jan. 11, 1498, it anchored for five days near the mouth of a small river between Natal and Mozambique, which they called the Rio do Cobre (Copper River). On January 25, in what is now Mozambique, they reached the Quelimane River, which they called the Rio dos Bons Sinais (the River of Good Omens), and erected another *padrão*. By this time many of the crews were sick with scurvy; the expedition rested a month while the ships were repaired.

On March 2 the fleet reached the Island of Mozambique, the inhabitants of which believed the Portuguese to be Muslims like themselves. Da Gama learned that they traded with Arab merchants and that four Arab vessels laden with gold, jewels, silver, and spices were then in port; he was also told that Prester John, the long-sought Christian ruler, lived in the interior but held many coastal cities. The Sultan of Mozambique supplied

Vasco de Gama is shown making a great show of presenting gifts to a feudal leader in India. Stock Montage/Archive Photos/Getty Images

da Gama with two pilots, one of whom deserted when he discovered that the Portuguese were Christians. The expedition reached Mombasa (now in Kenya) on April 7 and dropped anchor at Malindi (also now in Kenya) on April 14, where a Gujarati pilot who knew the route to Calicut, on the southwest coast of India, was taken aboard. After a 23-day run across the Indian Ocean, the Ghats Mountains of India were sighted, and Calicut was reached on May 20. There da Gama erected a *padrão* to prove he had reached India. The welcome of the Zamorin, the Hindu ruler, of Calicut (then the most important trading centre of southern India), was dispelled by da Gama's insignificant gifts and rude behaviour. Da Gama failed to conclude a treaty—partly because of the hostility of Muslim merchants and partly because the trumpery presents and cheap trade goods that he had brought, while suited to the West African trade, were hardly in demand in India. The Portuguese had mistakenly believed the Hindus to be Christians.

After tension increased, da Gama left at the end of August, taking with him five or six Hindus so that King Manuel might learn about their customs. Ignorance and indifference to local knowledge had led da Gama to choose the worst possible time of year for his departure, and he had to sail against the monsoon. He visited Anjidiv Island (near Goa) before sailing for Malindi, which he reached on Jan. 8, 1499, after nearly three months crossing the Arabian Sea. Many of the crew died of scurvy. At Malindi, because of greatly reduced numbers, da Gama ordered the *São Rafael* to be burned; there he also erected a *padrão*. Mozambique, where he set up his last *padrão*, was reached on February 1. On March 20 the *São Gabriel* and *Berrio* rounded the Cape together but a month later were parted by a storm; the *Berrio* reached the Tagus River in Portugal on July 10. Da Gama, in the *São Gabriel*, continued to Terceira Island in the Azores, whence he is said to have dispatched his flagship to Lisbon. He himself reached Lisbon on September 9 and made his triumphal entry nine days later, spending the interval mourning his brother Paulo, who had died on Terceira. (Out of da Gama's original crew of 170, only 55 men had survived.) Manuel I granted da Gama the title of *dom*, an annual pension of 1,000 cruzados, and estates.

THE SECOND VOYAGE

To exploit da Gama's achievement, Manuel I dispatched the Portuguese navigator Pedro Álvares Cabral to Calicut with a fleet of 13 ships. The profits of this expedition were such that a third fleet was soon fitted out in Lisbon. The command of this fleet was given to da Gama, who in January 1502 received the title of admiral. Da Gama commanded 10 ships, which were in turn supported by two flotillas of five ships each, each flotilla being under the command of one of his relations. Sailing in February 1502, the fleet called at the Cape Verdes, reaching the port of Sofala in East Africa on June 14. After calling briefly at Mozambique, the Portuguese expedition sailed to Kilwa, in what is now Tanzania. The ruler of Kilwa, the amīr Ibrāhīm, had been unfriendly to Cabral; da Gama threatened to burn Kilwa if the Amīr did not submit to the Portuguese and swear loyalty to King Manuel, which he then did.

Coasting southern Arabia, da Gama then called at Goa (later the focus of Portuguese power in India) before proceeding to Cannanore, a port in southwestern India to the north of Calicut, where he lay in wait for Arab shipping. After several days an Arab ship arrived with merchandise and between 200 and 400 passengers, including women and children. After seizing the cargo, da Gama is said to have shut up the passengers aboard the captured ship and set it afire, killing all on board. As a consequence, da Gama has been vilified, and Portuguese trading methods have been associated with terror. However, the episode is related only by late and unreliable sources and may be legendary or at least exaggerated.

After da Gama formed an alliance with the ruler of Cannanore, an enemy of the Zamorin, the fleet sailed to Calicut, with the aim of wrecking its trade and punishing the Zamorin for the favour he had shown to Muslim traders. Da Gama bombarded the port and seized and massacred 38 hostages. The Portuguese then sailed south to the port of Cochin, with whose ruler (an enemy of the

Zamorin) they formed an alliance. After an invitation to da Gama from the Zamorin had proved to be an attempt to entrap him, the Portuguese had a brief fight with Arab ships off Calicut but put them to full flight. On Feb. 20, 1503, the fleet left Cannanore for Mozambique on the first stage of their return voyage, reaching the Tagus on October 11.

THE THIRD VOYAGE

Obscurity surrounds the reception of da Gama on his return by King Manuel. Da Gama seemingly felt himself inadequately recompensed for his pains. Controversy broke out between the Admiral and the Order of São Tiago over the ownership of the town of Sines, which the Admiral had been promised but which the order refused to yield. Da Gama had married a lady of good family, Caterina de Ataíde—perhaps in 1500 after his return from his first voyage—and he then appears to have retired to the town of Évora. He was later granted additional privileges and revenues, and his wife bore him six sons. Until 1505 he continued to advise the King on Indian matters, and he was created count of Vidigueira in 1519. Not until after King Manuel died was he again sent overseas; King John III nominated him in 1524 as Portuguese viceroy in India.

Arriving in Goa in September 1524, da Gama immediately set himself to correct the many administrative abuses that had crept in under his predecessors. Whether from overwork or other causes, he soon fell ill and died in Cochin in December. In 1538 his body was taken back to Portugal.

PEDRO ÁLVARES CABRAL

(b. 1467/68, Belmonte, Portugal—d. 1520, Santarém?),
    Pedro Álvares Cabral was a Portuguese navigator who is generally credited as the discoverer of Brazil (April 22, 1500).

The son of Fernão Cabral, a nobleman, and of Isabel de Gouveia, Pedro Cabral was heir to a long tradition of service to the throne. He himself enjoyed the esteem of King Manuel I of Portugal, from whom he received various privileges in 1497; these included a personal allowance, the title of counselor to his highness, and the habit of the military Order of Christ. Three years later the king entrusted him with the command of the second major expedition to India, expressing "the great confidence we have in Pedralvares de Gouveia, nobleman of our household." Cabral was named admiral in supreme command of 13 ships, which set out from Lisbon on March 9, 1500. He was to follow the route taken earlier by Vasco da Gama, to strengthen commercial ties, and to further the conquest his predecessor had begun.

In accordance with da Gama's instructions, based on his experiences during the first voyage, Cabral was to sail southwest so as to bypass the becalmed waters of the Gulf of Guinea. This course, which later became known as the "circle around Brazil," had the added advantage of providing the Portuguese with opportunity to reconnoitre along the coast of the lands to the west, which they had previously sighted and which belonged to them in accordance with the Treaty of Tordesillas (1494).

Sailing westward under favourable conditions, on April 22, Cabral sighted the land he named Island of the True Cross. Later renamed Holy Cross by King Manuel, the country ultimately took its modern name, Brazil, from a kind of dyewood, *pau-brasil,* that is found there.Cabral is reported to have made a special effort to treat the inhabitants kindly, receiving them on board his caravel. Nonetheless, he took formal possession of the country and dispatched one of his ships to Portugal to inform the king. Henceforth, maps of the region showed Portugal as ruler of a great expanse of land with vaguely defined

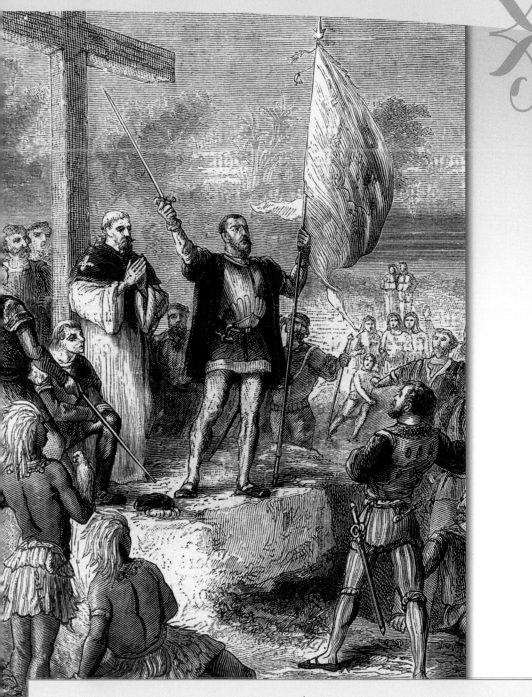

Artist's depiction of navigator Pedro Álvares Cabral claiming Brazil for Portugal. Apic/Hulton Archive/Getty Images

boundaries that came to serve as a point of call on the long voyage from Europe to the Cape of Good Hope and the Indian Ocean.

After a stay of only 10 days in Brazil, Cabral sailed for India, in a voyage that was plagued by a series of misfortunes. On May 29, while the fleet was rounding the Cape of Good Hope, four ships were lost with all hands aboard. The remaining ships cast anchor on Sept. 13, 1500, at Calicut, India, where the *zamorin* (Muslim ruler) welcomed Cabral and allowed him to establish a fortified trading post. Disputes with Muslim traders soon arose, however, and on December 17 a large Muslim force attacked the trading post. Most of the Portuguese defenders were killed before reinforcements could arrive from the Portuguese fleet lying at anchor in the harbour.

Cabral retaliated by bombarding the city, and then by capturing 10 Muslim vessels and executing their crews. He then sailed for the Indian port of Cochin, farther south, where he was affably received and permitted to trade for precious spices, with which he loaded his six remaining ships. Cabral also made port at Carangolos and Cananor on the same coast, completed his cargo, and on Jan. 16, 1501, began the return voyage to Portugal. On his way, however, two ships foundered, and it was with only four vessels that Cabral finally reached the mouth of the Tagus River in Portugal on June 23, 1501.

King Manuel was pleased at the outcome of the undertaking, in spite of the misfortunes that had beset it. He is said to have at first favoured making Cabral head of a new and more powerful expedition, but in the end it was Vasco da Gama and not Cabral who was appointed to that command. Accounts differ as to the reason for the king's change of heart. One chronicler attributes it to disagreement over division of authority within the new fleet; another offers the explanation that da Gama opposed the appointment of Cabral on the grounds that da Gama himself already held the title admiral of all the fleets that might leave Portugal for India and that the disasters of Cabral's expedition should disqualify him for the new mission.

Whatever the true explanation, Cabral held no further position of authority at the Portuguese court. He retired to his estate in the Beira Baixa province of Portugal and spent his remaining years there. His tomb at Santarém was identified in 1848 by the Brazilian historian Francisco Adolfo Varnhagen.

CHAPTER 4

WESTWARD WITH CHRISTOPHER COLUMBUS

C hristopher Columbus (Italian Cristoforo Colombo, Spanish Cristóbal Colón,), master navigator and admiral, undertook four transatlantic voyages (1492–93, 1493–96, 1498–1500, and 1502–04) that opened the way for European exploration, exploitation, and colonization of the Americas. He has long been called the "discoverer" of the New World, although Vikings such as Leif Eriksson had visited North America five centuries earlier.

Columbus made his transatlantic voyages under the sponsorship of Ferdinand II and Isabella I, the Catholic Monarchs of Aragon, Castile, and Leon in Spain. He was at first full of hope and ambition, an ambition partly gratified by his title "Admiral of the Ocean Sea," awarded to him in April 1492, and by the grants enrolled in the *Book of Privileges* (a record of his titles and claims). However, he died a disappointed man.

EARLY CAREER AND PREPARATION FOR THE FIRST VOYAGE

Little is known of Columbus's early life. The vast majority of scholars, citing Columbus's testament of 1498 and archival documents from Genoa and Savona, believe that he was born in Genoa between Aug. 26 and Oct. 31 in 1451

Portrait of Christopher Columbus, one of the most famous explorers from the Age of Discovery. Library of Congress Prints and Photographs Division

to a Christian household. However, it has been claimed that he was a converted Jew or that he was born in Spain, Portugal, or elsewhere. Columbus was the eldest son of Domenico Colombo, a Genoese wool worker and merchant, and Susanna Fontanarossa, his wife.

Columbus's career as a seaman began effectively in the Portuguese merchant marine. After surviving a shipwreck off Cape St. Vincent at the southwestern point of Portugal in 1476, he based himself in Lisbon, together with his brother Bartholomew. Both were employed as chart makers, but Christopher Columbus was principally a seagoing entrepreneur. In 1477 he sailed to Iceland and Ireland with the merchant marine, and in 1478 he was buying sugar in Madeira as an agent for the Genoese firm of Centurioni.

In 1479 he met and married Felipa Perestrello e Moniz, a member of an impoverished noble Portuguese family. Their son, Diego, was born in 1480. Between 1482 and 1485 Columbus traded along the Guinea and Gold coasts of tropical West Africa and made at least one voyage to the Portuguese fortress of São Jorge da Mina there, gaining knowledge of Portuguese navigation and the Atlantic wind systems along the way. Felipa died in 1485, and Columbus took as his mistress Beatriz Enríquez de Harana of Córdoba, by whom he had his second son, Ferdinand.

In 1484 Columbus began seeking support for an Atlantic crossing from King John II of Portugal but was denied aid. (Some conspiracy theorists have alleged that Columbus made a secret pact with the monarch, but there is no evidence of this.) By 1486 Columbus was firmly in Spain, asking for patronage from King Ferdinand and Queen Isabella. After at least two rejections, he at last obtained royal support in January 1492. This was achieved chiefly through the interventions of the Spanish treasurer, Luis de Santángel, and of the Franciscan friars of La Rábida, near Huelva, with whom Columbus had stayed in the summer of 1491. Juan Pérez of La Rábida had been one of the queen's confessors and perhaps procured him the crucial audience.

Christian missionary and anti-Islamic fervour, the power of Castile and Aragon, the fear of Portugal, the lust for gold, the desire for adventure, the hope of conquests, and Europe's genuine need for a reliable supply of herbs and spices for cooking, preserving, and medicine all combined to produce an explosion of energy that launched the first voyage. Columbus had been present at the siege of Granada, which was the last Moorish stronghold to fall to Spain (Jan. 2, 1492), and he was in fact riding back from Granada to La Rábida when he was recalled to the Spanish court and the vital royal audience. Granada's fall had produced euphoria among Spanish Christians and encouraged designs of ultimate triumph over the Islamic world, albeit chiefly, perhaps, by the back way round the globe. A direct assault eastward could prove difficult, because the Ottoman Empire and other Islamic states in the region had been gaining strength at a pace that was threatening the Christian monarchies themselves. The Islamic powers had effectively closed the land routes to the East and made the sea route south from the Red Sea extremely hard to access.

In the letter that prefaces his journal of the first voyage, the admiral vividly evokes his own hopes and binds them all together with the conquest of the infidel, the victory of Christianity, and the westward route to discovery and Christian alliance:

> ...and I saw the Moorish king come out of the gates of the city and kiss the royal hands of Your Highnesses... and Your Highnesses, as Catholic Christians...took thought to send me, Christopher Columbus, to the said parts of India, to see those princes and peoples

and lands...and the manner which should be used to bring about their conversion to our holy faith, and ordained that I should not go by land to the eastward, by which way it was the custom to go, but by way of the west, by which down to this day we do not know certainly that anyone has passed; therefore, having driven out all the Jews from your realms and lordships in the same month of January, Your Highnesses commanded me that, with a sufficient fleet, I should go to the said parts of India, and for this accorded me great rewards and ennobled me so that from that time henceforth I might style myself "Don" and be high admiral of the Ocean Sea and viceroy and perpetual Governor of the islands and continent which I should discover...and that my eldest son should succeed to the same position, and so on from generation to generation forever.

Thus a great number of interests were involved in this adventure, which was, in essence, the attempt to find a route to the rich land of Cathay (China), to India, and to the fabled gold and spice islands of the East by sailing westward over what was presumed to be open sea. Columbus himself clearly hoped to rise from his humble beginnings in this way, to accumulate riches for his family, and to join the ranks of the nobility of Spain. In a similar manner, but at a more exalted level, the Catholic Monarchs hoped that such an enterprise would gain them greater status among the monarchies of Europe, especially against their main rival, Portugal. Then, in alliance with the papacy (in this case, with the Borgia pope Alexander VI [1492–1503]), they might hope to take the lead in the Christian war against the infidel.

At a more elevated level still, Franciscan brethren were preparing for the eventual end of the world, as they believed was prophesied in the Revelation to John. According to that eschatological vision, Christendom would recapture Jerusalem and install a Christian emperor in the Holy Land as a precondition for the coming and defeat of Antichrist, the Christian conversion of the whole human race, and the Last Judgment. Franciscans and others hoped that Columbus's westward project would help to finance a Crusade to the Holy Land that might even be reinforced by, or coordinated with, offensives from the legendary ruler Prester John, who was thought to survive with his descendants in the lands to the east of the infidel. The emperor of Cathay—whom Europeans referred to as the Great Khan of the Golden Horde—was himself held to be interested in Christianity, and Columbus carefully carried a letter of friendship addressed to him by the Spanish monarchs. Finally, the Portuguese explorer Bartolomeu Dias was known to have pressed southward along the coast of West Africa, beyond São Jorge da Mina, in an effort to find an easterly route to Cathay and India by sea. It would never do to allow the Portuguese to find the sea route first.

THE FIRST VOYAGE

The ships for the first voyage—the *Niña*, *Pinta*, and *Santa María*—were fitted out at Palos, on the Tinto River in Spain. The little fleet left on Aug. 3, 1492. The admiral's navigational genius showed itself immediately, for they sailed southward to the Canary Islands, off the northwest African mainland, rather than sailing due west to the islands of the Azores. The westerlies prevailing in the Azores had defeated previous attempts to sail to the west, but in the Canaries the three ships could pick up the northeast trade winds; supposedly, they could trust to the westerlies for their return. After nearly a month in the Canaries the ships set out from San Sebastián de la Gomera on September 6.

On several occasions in September and early October, sailors spotted floating vegetation and various types of birds—all taken as signs that land was nearby. But by October 10 the crew had begun to lose patience, complaining that with their failure to make landfall, contrary winds and a shortage of provisions would keep them from returning home. Columbus allayed their fears, at least temporarily, and on October 12 land was sighted from the *Pinta* (though Columbus, on the *Niña*, later claimed the privilege for himself). The place of the first Caribbean landfall, called Guanahani, is hotly disputed, but San Salvador (Watlings) Island in the Bahamas is generally preferred to other Bahamian islands (Samana Cay, Rum Cay, or the Plana Cays) or to the Turks and Caicos Islands. Beyond

Residents of San Salvador Island in the Bahamas walking past a cross marking the spot where Christopher Columbus purportedly made his first Caribbean landfall. B. Anthony Stewart/National Geographic Image Collection/Getty Images

planting the royal banner, however, Columbus spent little time there, being anxious to press on to Cipango, or
Cipangu (Japan). He thought that he had found it in Cuba,
where he landed on October 28, but he convinced himself
by November 1 that Cuba was the Cathay mainland itself,
though he had yet to see evidence of great cities. Thus,
on December 5, he turned back southeastward to search
for the fabled city of Zaiton (Quanzhou, China), missing
through this decision his sole chance of setting foot on
Florida soil.

Adverse winds carried the fleet to an island called Ayti
(Haiti) by its Taino inhabitants; on December 6 Columbus
renamed it La Isla Española, or Hispaniola. He seems to
have thought that Hispaniola might be Cipango or, if not
Cipango, then perhaps one of the legendarily rich isles
from which King Solomon's triennial fleet brought back
gold, gems, and spices to Jerusalem (1 Kings 10:11, 22);
alternatively, he reasoned that the island could be related
to the biblical kingdom of Sheba (Saba'). There Columbus
found at least enough gold and prosperity to save him from
ridicule on his return to Spain. With the help of a Taino
cacique, or Indian chief, named Guacanagarí, he set up a
stockade on the northern coast of the island, named it La
Navidad, and posted 39 men to guard it until his return.
The accidental running aground of the *Santa María* provided additional planks and provisions for the garrison.

On Jan. 16, 1493, Columbus left with his remaining
two ships for Spain. The journey back was a nightmare.
The westerlies did indeed direct them homeward, but in
mid-February a terrible storm engulfed the fleet. The *Niña*
was driven to seek harbour at Santa Maria in the Azores,
where Columbus led a pilgrimage of thanksgiving to the
shrine of the Virgin; however, hostile Portuguese authorities temporarily imprisoned the group. After securing
their freedom Columbus sailed on, stormbound, and the

damaged ship limped to port in Lisbon. There he was obliged to interview with King John II. These events left Columbus under the suspicion of collaborating with Spain's enemies and cast a shadow on his return to Palos on March 15.

On this first voyage many tensions built up that were to remain through all of Columbus's succeeding efforts. First and perhaps most damaging of all, the admiral's apparently high religious and even mystical aspirations were incompatible with the realities of trading, competition, and colonization. Columbus never openly acknowledged this gulf and so was quite incapable of bridging it. The admiral also adopted a mode of sanctification and autocratic leadership that made him many enemies. Moreover, Columbus was determined to take back both material and human cargo to his sovereigns and for himself, and this could be accomplished only if his sailors carried on looting, kidnapping, and other violent acts, especially on Hispaniola. Although he did control some of his men's excesses, these developments blunted his ability to retain the high moral ground and the claim in particular that his "discoveries" were divinely ordained. Further, the Spanish court revived its latent doubts about the foreigner Columbus's loyalty to Spain, and some of Columbus's companions set themselves against him. Captain Pinzón had disputed the route as the fleet reached the Bahamas; he had later sailed the *Pinta* away from Cuba, and Columbus, on November 21, failing to rejoin him until January 6. The *Pinta* made port at Bayona on its homeward journey, separately from Columbus and the *Niña*. Had Pinzón not died so soon after his return, Columbus's command of the second voyage might have been less than assured. As it was, the Pinzón family became his rivals for reward.

THE SECOND AND THIRD VOYAGES

The gold, parrots, spices, and human captives Columbus displayed for his sovereigns at Barcelona convinced all of the need for a rapid second voyage. Columbus was now at the height of his popularity, and he led at least 17 ships out from Cádiz on Sept. 25, 1493. Colonization and Christian evangelization were openly included this time in the plans, and a group of friars shipped with him. The presence of some 1,300 salaried men with perhaps 200 private investors and a small troop of cavalry are testimony to the anticipations for the expedition.

Sailing again via Gomera in the Canary Islands, the fleet took a more southerly course than on the first voyage and reached Dominica in the Lesser Antilles on November 3. After sighting the Virgin Islands, it entered Samaná Bay in Hispaniola on November 23. Michele de Cuneo, deeply impressed by this unerring return, remarked that "since Genoa was Genoa there was never born a man so well equipped and expert in navigation as the said lord Admiral."

An expedition to Navidad four days later was shocked to find the stockade destroyed and the men dead. Here was a clear sign that Taino resistance had gathered strength. More fortified places were rapidly built, including a city, founded on January 2 and named La Isabela for the queen. On February 2 Antonio de Torres left La Isabela with 12 ships, some gold, spices, parrots, and captives (most of whom died en route), as well as the bad news about Navidad and some complaints about Columbus's methods of government. While Torres headed for Spain, two of Columbus's subordinates, Alonso de Ojeda and Pedro Margarit, took revenge for the massacre at Navidad and captured slaves. In March Columbus explored the Cibao Valley (thought to be the gold-bearing region of the island)

and established the fortress of St. Thomas (Santo Tomás) there. Then, late in April, Columbus led the *Niña* and two other ships to explore the Cuban coastline and search for gold in Jamaica, only to conclude that Hispaniola promised the richest spoils for the settlers. The admiral decided that Hispaniola was indeed the biblical land of Sheba and that Cuba was the mainland of Cathay. On June 12, 1494, Columbus insisted that his men swear a declaration to that effect—an indication that he intended to convince his sovereign he had reached Cathay, though not all of Columbus's company agreed with him. The following year he began a determined conquest of Hispaniola, spreading devastation among the Taino. There is evidence, especially in the objections of a friar, Bernardo Buil, that Columbus's methods remained harsh.

The admiral departed La Isabela for Spain on March 10, 1496, leaving his brothers, Bartholomew and Diego, in charge of the settlement. He reached Cádiz on June 11 and immediately pressed his plans for a third voyage upon his sovereigns, who were at Burgos. Spain was then at war with France and needed to buy and keep its alliances; moreover, the yield from the second voyage had fallen well short of the investment. Portugal was still a threat, though the two nations had divided the Atlantic conveniently between themselves in the Treaty of Tordesillas (June 7, 1494). According to the treaty, Spain might take all land west of a line drawn from pole to pole 370 leagues— i.e., about 1,910 km (1,185 miles)—west of the Cape Verde Islands, whereas Portugal could claim land to the east of the line. But what about the other side of the world, where West met East? Also, there might be a previously undiscovered antipodean continent. Who, then, should be trusted to draw the line there? Ferdinand and Isabella therefore made a cautious third investment. Six ships left Sanlúcar de Barrameda on May 30, 1498, three filled with explorers and three with provisions for the settlement on Hispaniola. It was clear now that Columbus was expected both to find great prizes and to establish the flag of Spain firmly in the East.

Certainly he found prizes, but not quite of the kind his sponsors required. His aim was to explore to the south of the existing discoveries, in the hope of finding both a strait from Cuba (his "Cathay") to India and, perhaps, the unknown antipodean continent. On June 21 the provision ships left Gomera for Hispaniola, while the explorers headed south for the Cape Verde Islands. Columbus began the Atlantic crossing on July 4 from São Tiago Island in Cape Verde. He discovered the principle of compass variation (the variation at any point on the Earth's surface between the direction to magnetic and geographic north), for which he made brilliant allowance on the journey from Margarita Island to Hispaniola on the later leg of this voyage, and he also observed, though misunderstood, the diurnal rotation of the northern polestar (Polaris). After stopping at Trinidad (named for the Holy Trinity, whose protection he had invoked for the voyage), Columbus entered the Gulf of Paria and planted the Spanish flag on the Paria Peninsula in Venezuela. He sent the caravel *El Corréo* southward to investigate the mouth of the Grande River (a northern branch of the Orinoco River delta), and by August 15 he knew by the great torrents of fresh water flowing into the Gulf of Paria that he had discovered another continent—"another world." But he did not find the strait to India, nor did he find King Solomon's gold mines, which his reading had led him and his sovereigns to expect in these latitudes; and he made only disastrous discoveries when he returned to Hispaniola.

Both the Taino and the European immigrants had resented the rule of Bartholomew and Diego Columbus. A rebellion by the mayor of La Isabela, Francisco Roldán, had led to appeals to the Spanish court, and, even as Columbus attempted to restore order (partly by hangings), the Spanish chief justice, Francisco de Bobadilla, was on his way to the colony with a royal commission to investigate the complaints. It is hard to explain exactly what the trouble was. Columbus's report to his sovereigns from the second voyage, taken back by Torres and so known as the Torres Memorandum, speaks of sickness, poor provisioning, recalcitrant natives, and undisciplined *hidalgos* (gentry). It may be that these problems had intensified. But the Columbus family must be held at least partly responsible, intent as it was on enslaving the Taino and shipping them to Europe or forcing them to mine gold on Hispaniola. Under Columbus's original system of gold production, local chiefs had been in charge

Illustration depicting Columbus in shackles on the deck of La Gorda *following his expulsion from Hispanola in 1500.* Library of Congress Prints and Photographs Division

of delivering gold on a loose per capita basis; the *adelantado* (governor) Bartholomew Columbus had replaced that policy with a system of direct exploitation led by favoured Spaniards, causing widespread dissent among unfavoured Spaniards and indigenous chiefs. Bobadilla ruled against the Columbus family when he arrived in Hispaniola. He clapped Columbus and his two brothers in irons and sent them promptly back on the ship *La Gorda*, and they arrived at Cádiz in late October 1500.

During that return journey Columbus composed a long letter to his sovereigns that is one of the most extraordinary he wrote, and one of the most informative. One part of its exalted, almost mystical, quality may be attributed to the humiliations the admiral had endured (humiliations he compounded by refusing to allow the captain of the *La Gorda* to remove his chains during the voyage) and another to the fact that he was now suffering severely from sleeplessness, eyestrain, and a form of rheumatoid arthritis, which may have hastened his death. Much of what he said in the letter, however, seems genuinely to have expressed his beliefs. It shows that Columbus had absolute faith in his navigational abilities, his seaman's sense of the weather, his eyes, and his reading. He asserted that he had reached the outer region of the Earthly Paradise, in that, during his earlier approach to Trinidad and the Paria Peninsula, the polestar's rotation had given him the impression that the fleet was climbing. The weather had become extremely mild, and the flow of fresh water into the Gulf of Paria was, as he saw, enormous. All this could have one explanation only—they had mounted toward the temperate heights of the Earthly Paradise, heights from which the rivers of Paradise ran into the sea. Columbus had found all such signs of the outer regions of the Earthly Paradise in his reading, and indeed they were widely known. On this estimate, he was therefore close to the realms of gold that lay near Paradise. He had not found the gold yet, to be sure, but he knew where it was. Columbus's expectations thus allowed him to interpret his discoveries in terms of biblical and Classical sources and to do so in a manner that would be comprehensible to his sponsors and favourable to himself.

This letter, desperate though it was, convinced the sovereigns that, even if he had not yet found the prize, he had been close to it after all. They ordered his release and gave him audience at Granada in late December 1500. They accepted that Columbus's capacities as navigator and explorer were unexcelled, although he was an unsatisfactory governor, and on Sept. 3, 1501, they appointed Nicolás de Ovando to succeed Bobadilla to the governorship. Columbus, though ill and importunate, was a better investment than the many adventurers and profiteers who had meantime been licensed to compete with him, and there was always the danger (revealed in some of the letters of this period) that he would offer his services to his native Genoa. In October 1501 Columbus went to Sevilla to make ready his fourth and final expedition.

THE FOURTH VOYAGE AND FINAL YEARS

The winter and spring of 1501–02 were exceedingly busy. The four chosen ships were bought, fitted, and crewed, and some 20 of Columbus's extant letters and memoranda were written then, many in exculpation of Bobadilla's charges, others pressing even harder the nearness of the Earthly Paradise and the need to reconquer Jerusalem. Columbus took to calling himself "Christbearer" in his letters and to using a strange and mystical signature, never satisfactorily explained. He began also, with all these thoughts and pressures in mind, to compile his *Book of Privileges*, which defends the titles and financial claims of the Columbus family, and his apocalyptic *Book of Prophecies*, which includes several biblical passages. The first compilation seems an odd companion to the second, yet both were closely linked in the admiral's own mind. He seems to have been certain that his mission was divinely guided. Thus, the loftiness of his spiritual aspirations increased as the threats to his personal ones mounted. In the midst of all these efforts and hazards, Columbus sailed from Cádiz on his fourth voyage on May 9, 1502.

Columbus's sovereigns had lost much of their confidence in him, and there is much to suggest that pity mingled with hope in their support. His four ships contrasted sharply with the 30 granted to the governor Ovando. His illnesses were worsening, and the hostility to his rule in Hispaniola was unabated. Thus, Ferdinand and Isabella forbade him to return there. He was to resume, instead, his interrupted exploration of the "other world" to the south that he had found on his third voyage and to look particularly for gold and the strait to India. Columbus expected to meet the Portuguese navigator Vasco da Gama in the East, and the sovereigns instructed him on the appropriate courteous behaviour for such a meeting— another sign, perhaps, that they did not wholly trust him.

They were right. He departed from Gran Canaria on the night of May 25, made landfall at Martinique on June 15 (after the fastest crossing to date), and was, by June 29, demanding entrance to Santo Domingo on Hispaniola. Only on being refused entry by Ovando did he sail away to the west and south. From July to September 1502 he explored the coast of Jamaica, the southern shore of Cuba, Honduras, and the Mosquito Coast of Nicaragua. His feat of Caribbean transnavigation, which took him to Bonacca Island off Cape Honduras on July 30, deserves to be reckoned on a par, as to difficulty, with that of crossing the Atlantic, and the admiral was justly proud of it.

The fleet continued southward along Costa Rica. Constantly probing for the strait, Columbus sailed round the Chiriquí Lagoon (in Panama) in October; then, searching for gold, he explored the Panamanian region of Veragua (Veraguas) in the foulest of weather. In order to exploit the promising gold yield he was beginning to find there, the admiral in February 1503 attempted to establish a trading post at Santa María de Belén on the bank of the Belén (Bethlehem) River under the command of Bartholomew Columbus. However, Indian resistance and the poor condition of his ships (of which only two remained, fearfully holed by shipworm) caused him to turn back to Hispaniola. On this voyage disaster again struck. Against Columbus's better judgment, his pilots turned the fleet north too soon. The ships could not make the distance and had to be beached on the coast of Jamaica. By June 1503 Columbus and his crews were castaways.

Columbus had hoped, as he said to his sovereigns, that "my hard and troublesome voyage may yet turn out to be my noblest"; it was in fact the most disappointing of all and the most unlucky. In its explorations the fleet had missed discovering the Pacific (across the isthmus of Panama) and failed to make contact with the Maya of Yucatán by the narrowest of margins. Two of the men—Diego Méndez and Bartolomeo Fieschi, captains of the wrecked ships *La Capitana* and *Vizcaíno*, respectively—left about July 17 by canoe to get help for the castaways; although they managed to traverse the 720 km (450 miles) of open sea to Hispaniola, Ovando made no great haste to deliver that help. In the meantime, the admiral displayed his acumen once again by correctly predicting an eclipse of the Moon from his astronomical tables, thus frightening the local peoples into providing food; but rescuers did not arrive until June 1504, and Columbus and his men did not reach Hispaniola until August 13 of that year. On November 7 he

Stranded on the island of Jamaica during his disastrous final voyage, Columbus convinced the natives to help him and his crew by predicting a lunar eclipse. Frederic Lewis/Archive Photos/Getty Images

sailed back to Sanlúcar and found that Queen Isabella, his main supporter, had made her will and was dying.

Columbus always maintained that he had found the true Indies and Cathay in the face of mounting evidence that he had not. Perhaps he genuinely believed that he had been there; in any event, his disallowances of the "New World" hindered his goals of nobility and wealth and dented his later reputation. Columbus had been remote from his companions and intending colonists, and he had been a poor judge of the ambitions, and perhaps the failings, of those who sailed with him. This combination proved damaging to almost all of his hopes. Nonetheless, it would be wrong to suppose that Columbus spent his final two years wholly in illness, poverty, and oblivion. His son Diego was well established at court, and the admiral himself lived in Sevilla in some style. His "tenth" of the gold diggings in Hispaniola, guaranteed in 1493, provided a substantial revenue (against which his Genoese bankers allowed him to draw), and one of the few ships to escape a hurricane off Hispaniola in 1502 (in which Bobadilla himself went down) was that carrying Columbus's gold. He felt himself ill-used and shortchanged nonetheless, and these years were marred, for both him and King Ferdinand, by his constant pressing for redress. Columbus followed the court from Segovia to Salamanca and Valladolid, attempting to gain an audience. He knew that his life was nearing its end, and in August 1505 he began to amend his will. He died on May 20, 1506, in Valladolid. First he was laid in the Franciscan friary there, then taken to the family mausoleum established at the Carthusian monastery of Las Cuevas in Sevilla. In 1542, by the will of his son Diego, Columbus's bones were laid with his own in the Cathedral of Santo Domingo, Hispaniola (now in the Dominican Republic). After Spain ceded Hispaniola to France, the remains were moved to Havana, Cuba, in 1795 and returned to Sevilla in 1898. In 1877, however, workers at the cathedral in Santo Domingo claimed to have found another set of bones that were marked as those of Columbus. Since 1992 these bones have been interred in the Columbus Lighthouse (Faro a Colón).

ASSESSMENT

The period between the quatercentenary celebrations of Columbus's achievements in 1892–93 and the quincentenary ones of 1992 saw great advances in Columbus scholarship. Numerous books about Columbus appeared

COLUMBUS'S SMALL WORLD

Contrary to common lore, Columbus never thought that the world was flat. Educated Europeans had known that the Earth was spherical in shape since at least the early 7th century, when the popular *Etymologies of St. Isidore of Sevilla* were produced in Spain. Columbus's miscalculations, such as they were, lay in other areas. First, his estimate of the sea distance to be crossed to Cathay was wildly inaccurate. Columbus rejected Ptolemy's estimate of the journey from West to East overland, substituting a far longer one based on a chart (now lost) supplied by the Florentine mathematician and geographer Paolo Toscanelli, and on Columbus's preference for the calculations of the Classical geographer Marinus of Tyre. Additionally, Columbus's reading primarily of the 13th–14th-century Venetian Marco Polo's *Travels* gave him the idea that the lands of the East stretched out far around the back of the globe, with the island of Cipango—itself surrounded by islands—located a further 2,400 km (1,500 miles) from the mainland of Cathay. He seems to have argued that this archipelago might be near the Azores.

Columbus also read the seer Salathiel-Ezra in the books of Esdras, from the Apocrypha (especially 2 Esdras 6:42, in which the prophet states that the Earth is six parts land to one of water), thus reinforcing these ideas of the proportion of land-to sea-crossing. The mistake was further compounded by his idiosyncratic view of the length of a degree of geographic latitude. The degree, according to Arabic calculators, consisted of 5623 Arab miles, and an Arab mile measured 6,481 feet (1,975.5 metres). Given that a nautical mile measures 6,076 feet (1,852 metres), this degree amounts to approximately 60.45 nautical miles (112 km). Columbus, however, used the Italian mile of 4,847 feet (1,477.5 metres) for his computations and thus arrived at approximately 45 nautical miles (83 km) to a degree. This shortened the supposed distance across the sea westward to such an extent that Zaiton, Marco Polo's great port of Cathay, would have lain a little to the east of present-day San Diego, California, U.S. Also, the islands of Cipango would have been about as far north of the Equator as the Virgin Islands — close to where Columbus actually made his landfalls.

The miscalculation of distance may have been willful on Columbus's part and made with an eye to his sponsors. The journal he kept in his first voyage suggests that Columbus may have been aware of his inaccuracy, for he consistently concealed from his sailors the great number of miles they had covered, lest they become fearful for the journey back. Such manipulations may be interpreted as evidence of bravery and the need to inspire confidence rather than of simple dishonesty or error.

in the 1990s, and the insights of archaeologists and anthropologists began to complement those of sailors and historians. This effort has given rise, as might be expected, to considerable debate. There has also been a major shift in approach and interpretation; the older pro-European understanding has given way to one shaped from the perspective of the inhabitants of the Americas themselves. According to the older understanding, the "discovery" of the Americas was a great triumph, one in which Columbus played the part of hero in accomplishing the four voyages, in being the means of bringing great material profit to Spain and to other European countries, and in opening up the Americas to European settlement. The more recent perspective, however, has concentrated on the destructive side of the European conquest, emphasizing, for example, the disastrous impact of the slave trade and the ravages of imported disease on the indigenous peoples of the Caribbean region and the American continents. The sense of triumph has diminished accordingly, and the view of Columbus as hero has now been replaced, for many, by one of a man deeply flawed.

The pendulum may, however, have swung too far. Columbus has been blamed for events far beyond his own reach or knowledge, and too little attention has been paid to the historical circumstances that conditioned him. His obsessions with lineage and imperialism, his zealous religious beliefs, his enslaving of indigenous peoples, and his execution of colonial subjects come from a world remote from that of modern democratic ideas, but it was the world to which he belonged. The forces of European expansion, with their slaving and search for gold, had been unleashed before him and were quite beyond his control; he simply decided to be in their vanguard. He succeeded. Columbus's towering stature as a seaman and navigator, the sheer power of his religious convictions (self-delusory as they sometimes were), his personal magnetism, his courage, his endurance, his determination, and, above all, his achievements as an explorer should continue to be recognized.

CHAPTER 5

OTHER WESTWARD NAVIGATORS

Following the initial discoveries of Columbus, other navigators such as the Italians John Cabot, Sebastian Cabot, and Amerigo Vespucci explored the new lands at greater length, extending Europe's knowledge of what lay across the Atlantic. Finally, the Portuguese explorer Ferdinand Magellan, sailing under the flag of Spain, rounded the great southern continent and crossed the vast Pacific Ocean. His voyage around the world was completed by a Basque, Juan Sebastián del Cano, effectively bringing to a close the great Age of Discovery.

JOHN CABOT

(b. *c.* 1450, Genoa? [Italy]—d. *c.* 1499)

John Cabot (Italian Giovanni Caboto) was a navigator and explorer who by his voyages in 1497 and 1498 helped lay the groundwork for the later British claim to Canada. The exact details of his life and of his voyages are still subjects of controversy among historians and cartographers.

Cabot moved to Venice in 1461, or possibly earlier, and became a citizen of that city in 1476. While employed by a Venetian mercantile firm, he traveled to the eastern shores of the Mediterranean and visited Mecca, a great trading centre where Eastern and Western goods were exchanged.

Statue of John Cabot in Bristol, England. Cabot's voyages established British claims to Canada. Bob Cheung/Shutterstock.com

He became skilled in navigational techniques and seems to have envisaged, independently of Christopher Columbus, the possibility of reaching Asia by sailing westward.

Cabot's whereabouts and activities from the mid-1480s to the mid-1490s are in doubt, but it is believed that he moved with his family to England and had taken up residence in Bristol by the end of 1495. On March 5, 1496, King Henry VII of England issued letters patent to Cabot and his sons, authorizing them to voyage in search of unknown lands, to return their merchandise by the port of Bristol, and to enjoy a monopoly of any trade they might establish there. The news of Columbus's recent discoveries on behalf of Spain was a spur to English action and secured some support for Cabot from Bristol merchants.

In 1496 Cabot made a voyage from Bristol with one ship, but he was forced to turn back because of a shortage of food, inclement weather, and disputes with his crew. In May 1497, however, he set sail from Bristol in the small ship *Matthew*, with a crew of 18 men. He proceeded around Ireland and then north and west, making landfall on the morning of June 24. The exact landing place has never been definitely established: it has been variously believed to be in southern Labrador, Newfoundland, or Cape Breton Island. On going ashore, he noticed signs indicating that the area was inhabited but saw no people. Taking possession of the land for the English king, he unfurled both the English and Venetian flags. He conducted explorations from the ship along the coastline, naming various features Cape Discovery, Island of St. John, St. George's Cape, the Trinity Islands, and England's Cape. These may be, respectively, the present Cape North, St. Paul Island, Cape Ray, St. Pierre and Miquelon, and Cape Race, all in the area of Cabot Strait.

In the mistaken belief that he had reached the northeast coast of Asia, Cabot returned to Bristol on Aug. 6, 1497. He reported that the land was excellent, the climate temperate, and the sea covered with enough fish to end England's dependence on Iceland's fish. In the midst of an enthusiastic welcome, he announced his plans to return to his landing place and from there sail westward until he came to Japan, the reputed source of spices and gems. On

Feb. 3, 1498, he received new letters patent for a second expedition. Cabot's second expedition probably consisted of five ships and about 200 men. Soon after setting out in 1498, one ship was damaged and sought anchorage in Ireland, suggesting that the fleet had been hit by a severe storm. By 1499 Cabot had been given up for dead.

The effect of Cabot's efforts was to demonstrate the viability of a short route across the North Atlantic. This would later prove important in the establishment of British colonies in North America.

SEBASTIAN CABOT

(b. *c.* 1476, Bristol, Gloucestershire, England, or Venice — d. 1557, London)

Sebastian Cabot was a navigator, explorer, and cartographer who at various times served the English and Spanish crowns. He may have accompanied his father, John Cabot, on the first English voyage to North America (1497), which resulted in the discovery of the Labrador coast of Newfoundland (mistaken at the time for the coast of China).

Although facts concerning his early life remain obscure, Cabot was a cartographer to King Henry VIII in 1512, when he accompanied the English army sent to aid King Ferdinand II of Aragon against the French. Because of his knowledge of the northeast coast of North America, he was commissioned a captain in the Spanish navy, but Ferdinand's death canceled a voyage he was to command in 1516. His services were retained by the Holy Roman emperor Charles V, and in 1518 he was given membership in the Spanish Council of the New Indies and appointed pilot major and official examiner of pilots.

Cabot returned to England in 1520 and was offered a naval command but in 1525 assumed charge of a three-ship

Spanish expedition that was to develop trade with the East. He diverted the expedition from this objective, however, because of reports of fabulous wealth in the Río de la Plata region of South America. After about three years of fruitless exploration he returned to Spain, was judged responsible for the failure of the expedition, and was banished to Africa. Pardoned two years later, he was restored to his old post of pilot major. A copy of his well-known map of the world (1544) is in the Bibliothèque Nationale, Paris.

Offered a naval post in England by King Edward VI, Cabot accepted the appointment (1548) and was also pensioned. He remained in England as governor of the Merchant Adventurers (a company of influential English merchants), organizing an expedition to search for a northeast passage from Europe to Asia. Although this objective was not attained, and several naval disasters ensued, trade with Russia was facilitated.

AMERIGO VESPUCCI

(b. 1454?, Florence, Italy—d. 1512, Sevilla, Spain)
Amerigo Vespucci was a merchant and explorer-navigator who took part in early voyages to the New World (1499–1500, 1501–02). He occupied the influential post of *piloto mayor* ("master navigator") in Sevilla (1508–12). The name for the Americas is derived from his given name.

EARLY LIFE

Vespucci was the son of Nastagio, a notary. As a boy Vespucci was given a humanistic education by his uncle Giorgio Antonio. In 1479 he accompanied another relation, sent by the famous Italian Medici family to be their spokesman to the king of France. On returning,

Amerigo Vespucci, who went from outfitting voyages of Columbus to navigating his own voyages of exploration to America. Hulton Archive/ Getty Images

Vespucci entered the "bank" of Lorenzo and Giovanni di Pierfrancesco de' Medici and gained the confidence of his employers. At the end of 1491 their agent, Giannotto Berardi, appears to have been engaged partly in fitting out ships, and Vespucci was probably present when Christopher Columbus returned from his first expedition, which Berardi had assisted. Later Vespucci was to collaborate, still with Berardi, in the preparation of a ship for Columbus's second expedition and of others for his third. When Berardi died, either at the end of 1495 or at the beginning of 1496, Vespucci became manager of the Sevilla agency.

VESPUCCI'S VOYAGES

The period during which Vespucci made his voyages falls between 1497 and 1504. Two series of documents on his voyages are extant. The first series consists of a letter in the name of Vespucci from Lisbon, Portugal, dated Sept. 4, 1504, written in Italian, perhaps to the *gonfalonier* (magistrate of a medieval Italian republic) Piero Soderini, and printed in Florence in 1505; and of two Latin versions of this letter, printed under the titles of "Quattuor Americi navigationes" and "Mundus Novus," or "Epistola Alberici de Novo Mundo." The second series consists of three private letters addressed to the Medici. In the first series of documents, four voyages by Vespucci are mentioned; in the second, only two. Until the 1930s the documents of the first series were considered from the point of view of the order of the four voyages. According to a theory of Alberto Magnaghi, on the contrary, these documents are to be regarded as the result of skillful manipulations, and the sole authentic papers would be the private letters, so that the verified voyages would be reduced to two. The question is fundamental for the evaluation of Vespucci's work and has given rise to fierce controversy; attempts to reconcile the two series of documents cannot generally be considered successful.

The voyage completed by Vespucci between May 1499 and June 1500 as navigator of an expedition of four ships sent from Spain under the command of Alonso de Ojeda is certainly authentic. (This is the second expedition of the traditional series.) Since Vespucci took part as navigator, he certainly cannot have been inexperienced; but it does not seem possible that he had made a previous voyage (1497–98) in this area (i.e., around the Gulf of Mexico and the Atlantic coast from Florida to Chesapeake Bay), though this matter remains unresolved.

In the voyage of 1499–1500 Vespucci would seem to have left Ojeda after reaching the coast of what is now Guyana. Turning south, he is believed to have discovered the mouth of the Amazon River and to have gone as far as Cape St. Augustine (latitude about 6° S). On the way back he reached Trinidad, sighted the mouth of the Orinoco River, and then made for Haiti. Vespucci thought he had sailed along the coast of the extreme easterly peninsula of Asia, where Ptolemy, the geographer, believed the market of Cattigara to be; so he looked for the tip of this peninsula, calling it Cape Cattigara. He supposed that the ships, once past this point, emerged into the seas of southern Asia. As soon as he was back in Spain, he equipped a fresh expedition with the aim of reaching the Indian Ocean, the Gulf of the Ganges (modern Bay of Bengal), and the island of Taprobane or Ceylon (now Sri Lanka). But the Spanish government did not welcome his proposals, and at the end of 1500 Vespucci went into the service of Portugal.

Under Portuguese auspices Vespucci completed a second expedition, which set off from Lisbon on May 13, 1501. After a halt at the Cape Verde Islands, the expedition traveled southwestward and reached the coast of Brazil toward Cape St. Augustine. The remainder of the voyage is disputed, but Vespucci claimed to have continued southward, and he may have sighted (January 1502) Guanabara Bay (Rio de Janeiro's bay) and sailed as far as the Río de la Plata, making Vespucci the first European to discover that estuary (Juan Díaz de Solís arrived there in 1516). The ships may have journeyed still farther south, along the coast of Patagonia (in present-day southern Argentina). The return route is unknown. Vespucci's ships anchored at Lisbon on July 22, 1502.

LATER LIFE AND REPUTATION

It is uncertain whether Vespucci took part in yet another expedition (1503–04) for the Portuguese government (it is said that he may have been with one under Gonzalo Coelho). In any case, this expedition contributed no fresh knowledge. Although Vespucci subsequently helped to prepare other expeditions, he never again joined one in person.

At the beginning of 1505 he was summoned to the court of Spain for a private consultation and, as a man of experience, was engaged to work for the famous Casa de Contratación de las Indias (Commercial House for the Indies), which had been founded two years before at Sevilla. In 1508 the house appointed him chief navigator, a post of great responsibility, which included the examination of the pilots' and ships' masters' licenses for voyages. He also had to prepare the official map of newly discovered lands and of the routes to them (for the royal survey), interpreting and coordinating all data that the captains were obliged to furnish. Vespucci, who had obtained Spanish citizenship, held this position until his death. His widow, Maria Cerezo, was granted a pension in recognition of her husband's great services.

FROM AMERIGO TO AMERICA

The voyage of Amerigo Vespucci in 1501–02 is of fundamental importance in the history of geographic discovery in that
Vespucci himself became convinced that the newly discovered
lands were not part of Asia but a new world. Indeed, in one of
his letters, published in 1504, Vespucci used the term "Mundus
Novus" ("New World") in referring to South America. The letter circulated from hand to hand, and a copy reached Martin
Waldseemüller, a German cartographer. Waldseemüller (also
spelled Waltzemüller or Walzenmüller) was born c. 1470 in
Radolfzell, Württemberg (now part of Germany). Educated
at Freiburg im Breisgau, Württemberg, Waldseemüller eventually moved to Saint-Dié, in Lorraine (now in France).
There in 1507 he printed a pamphlet titled *Cosmographiae*

World map by Martin Waldseemüller, 1507. Geography and
Map Division/The Library of Congress, Washington, D.C.

introductio (*Introduction to Cosmography*), in which he observed that "another fourth part [of the inhabited earth] had been discovered by Americus Vespucius," and suggested that the new land be named "ab Americo Inventore...quasi Americi terram sive Americam" ("from Amerigo the discoverer...as if it were the land of Americus or America").

The proposal is perpetuated in a large planisphere of Waldseemüller's, in which the name America appears for the first time, although applied only to South America. On the upper part of the map, with the hemisphere comprising the Old World, appears a picture of Ptolemy; on the part of the map with the New World hemisphere is a picture of Vespucci.

Waldseemüller's book was widely read, and the suggestion caught on. The extension of the name to North America, however, came later. Waldseemüller died at Saint-Dié, possibly between 1518 and 1521.

Some scholars have held Vespucci to be a usurper of the merits of others. Yet, despite the possibly deceptive claims made by him or advanced on his behalf, he was a genuine pioneer of Atlantic exploration and a vivid contributor to the early travel literature of the New World.

FERDINAND MAGELLAN

(b. *c.* 1480, Sabrosa or Porto?, Portugal—d. April 27, 1521, Mactan, Philippines)

Ferdinand Magellan (Portuguese Fernão de Magalhães, Spanish Fernando, or Hernando, de Magallanes,) was a Portuguese navigator and explorer who sailed under the flags of both Portugal (1505–13) and Spain (1519–21). From

Spain he sailed around South America, discovering the Strait of Magellan, and across the Pacific. Though he was killed in the Philippines, one of his ships continued westward to Spain, accomplishing the first circumnavigation of the Earth. The voyage was successfully terminated by the Basque navigator Juan Sebastián del Cano.

EARLY LIFE

Magellan was the son of Rui de Magalhães and Alda de Mesquita, members of the Portuguese nobility. At an early age he became a page to Queen Leonor, wife of John II (reigned 1481–95) and sister of Manuel I (reigned 1495–1521), in Lisbon. In early 1505 he enlisted in the fleet of Francisco de Almeida, first viceroy of Portuguese India, whose expedition King Manuel sent to check Muslim sea power along the African and Indian coasts and to establish a strong Portuguese presence in the Indian Ocean. During a naval engagement at Cannanore (now Kannur) on the Malabar Coast of India, Magellan is said by the chronicler Gaspar Correia (also spelled Corrêa) to have been wounded. Though Correia states that during this early period of his Indian service Magellan acquired considerable knowledge of navigation, little is known of Magellan's first years in the East until he appears among those sailing in November 1506 with Nuno Vaz Pereira to Sofala on the Mozambique coast, where the Portuguese had established a fort.

By 1507 Magellan was back in India. He took part, on February 2–3, 1509, in the great Battle of Diu, in which the Portuguese defeated a Muslim fleet and thereby gained supremacy over most of the Indian Ocean. Reaching Cochin (now Kochi, India) in the fleet of Diogo Lopes de Sequeira, he subsequently left for the Malay city-state of Malacca (now Melaka, Mal.). Magellan is mentioned

Portuguese explorer Ferdinand Magellan. Sailing under a Spanish flag, Magellan discovered a strait through South America that bears his name. Library of Congress Prints and Photographs Division

as being sent to warn the commander of the Portuguese ships in Malacca's waters of impending attack by Malays. During the subsequent fighting he saved the life of a Portuguese explorer, his close friend Francisco Serrão. (Serrão, possibly a relative of Magellan's, had sailed with Magellan to India in 1505.) Magellan attempted to return to Portugal afterward but was unsuccessful. At a council held at Cochin on Oct. 10, 1510, to decide on plans for retaking Goa—which the Portuguese had captured earlier in the year but then lost—he advised against taking large ships at that season. Nevertheless, the new Portuguese governor in India, Afonso de Albuquerque, did so, and the city fell to the Portuguese on November 24. Magellan's name does not appear among those who fought.

The Portuguese victories off the eastern coast of Africa and the western coast of India had broken Muslim power in the Indian Ocean, and the purpose of Almeida's expedition—to wrest from the Arabs the key points of sea trade—was almost accomplished. Yet without control of Malacca, their achievement was incomplete. At the end of June 1511, therefore, a fleet under Albuquerque left for Malacca, which fell after six weeks. This event, in which Magellan took part, was the crowning Portuguese victory in the East. Through Malacca passed the wealth of the East to the harbours of the West, and in command of the Malacca Strait the Portuguese held the key to the seas and ports of Malaysia. It remained only to explore the wealth-giving Moluccas (now part of Indonesia), the islands of spice. Accordingly, early in December 1511 they sailed on a voyage of reconnaissance, and after reaching Banda they returned with spice in 1512. The claim made by some that Magellan went on this voyage rests on unproven statements by Italian geographer Giovanni Battista Ramusio and Spanish historian Leonardo de Argensola, and the want of evidence argues against its acceptance. However, it is known that Magellan's friend Serrão was in command of one of the ships and that he later sent Magellan helpful information from the Moluccas about those islands.

By mid-1513 Magellan was back in Lisbon, but he soon joined the forces sent against the Moroccan stronghold of Azamor (Azemmour). In a skirmish that August he sustained a leg wound that caused him to limp for the rest of his life. Returning to Lisbon in November 1514, he asked King Manuel for a token increase in his pension as a reward. But unfounded reports of irregular conduct on his part had reached the king: after the siege of Azamor, Magellan was accused of having sold a portion of the war spoils back to the enemy. Refusing Magellan's request for a reward, Manuel ordered him back to Morocco. Early in 1516 Magellan renewed his petition; the king, refusing once more, told him he might offer his services elsewhere.

ALLEGIANCE TO SPAIN

Magellan therefore went to Spain, reaching Sevilla (Seville) on Oct. 20, 1517. He was joined in December by the Portuguese cosmographer Rui Faleiro and possibly by Rui's brother Francisco Faleiro. Magellan and Rui Faleiro journeyed to the court at Valladolid, where they offered their services to King Charles I (later, Holy Roman emperor Charles V). Magellan, until this point bearing the Portuguese name Fernão de Magalhães, henceforward became known by the Spanish version of his name— Fernando de Magallanes.

By the Treaty of Tordesillas (1494), all newly discovered and undiscovered territories east of a line of demarcation (370 leagues west of the Cape Verde Islands) were assigned to Portugal; all that lay west belonged to Spain. Magellan and Faleiro now proposed to sail west to give practical proof of their claim that the Spice Islands lay west of the

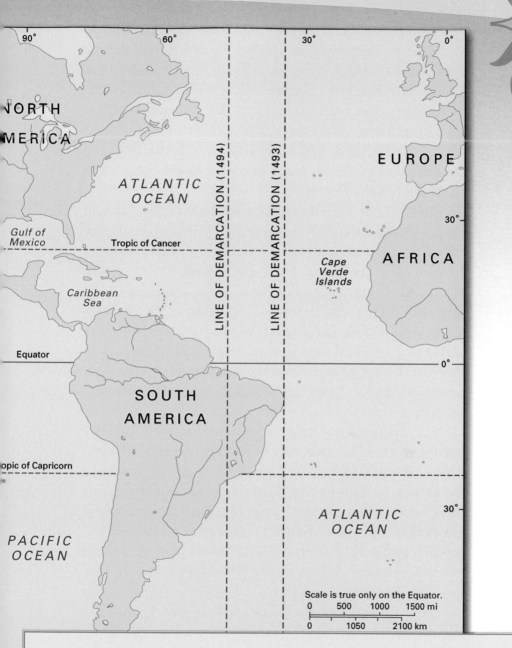

90° 60° 30° 0°

NORTH
AMERICA

ATLANTIC
OCEAN

EUROPE

Gulf of
Mexico

Tropic of Cancer

30°

LINE OF DEMARCATION (1494)

LINE OF DEMARCATION (1493)

AFRICA

Caribbean
Sea

Cape
Verde
Islands

Equator

0°

SOUTH
AMERICA

Tropic of Capricorn

ATLANTIC
OCEAN

30°

PACIFIC
OCEAN

Scale is true only on the Equator.

0   500   1000   1500 mi

0   1050   2100 km

Map showing the line of demarcation between Spanish and Portuguese territory, as first defined by Pope Alexander VI (1493) and later revised by the Treaty of Tordesillas (1494). Spain won control of lands discovered west of the line, while Portugal gained rights to new lands to the east. Encyclopædia Britannica, Inc.

line of demarcation—that is, within the Spanish, not the Portuguese, hemisphere. Magellan was convinced that he would lead his ships from the Atlantic to the "Sea of the South" by discovering a strait through Tierra Firme (the South American mainland). This idea did not originate with him; others had sought a passage by which vessels sailing continuously westward would reach the East and thus avoid the African Cape of Good Hope, which was controlled by the Portuguese.

On March 22, 1518, their proposal received royal assent. Magellan and Faleiro were appointed joint captains general of an expedition directed to seek an all-Spanish route to the Moluccas. In the royal agreement, Magellan and Faleiro were directed to find "the" strait, referring to the hypothetical passage through Tierra Firme. The government of any lands discovered was to be vested in them and their heirs, and they were to receive a one-twentieth share of the net profits from the venture. Both also were invested with the Order of Santiago, a Spanish military-religious knighthood.

The Spanish seafaring community reacted strongly against the king's acceptance of the Portuguese-led expedition. The influence of Juan Rodríguez de Fonseca, the bishop of Burgos and head of the powerful Casa de Contratación (House of Commerce), an administrative entity that oversaw all Spanish explorations, hindered the proper organization of the expedition, which was delayed more than once. Agents of the Portuguese crown, outraged by Magellan's transfer of allegiance, also made an unsuccessful attempt to wreck the project. Ultimately, the number of Portuguese sailors assigned to the expedition was strictly limited, Fonseca managed to install a Spanish officer as a sort of cocommander of the fleet, and Magellan lost his Portuguese cocaptain, Faleiro, whose mental instability prevented him from sailing. Conflicts between the Portuguese and Spanish officers on board would lead to severe discipline problems.

Spanish officials furnished five ships for the expedition, prepared in Sevilla. Magellan's flagship, the *Trinidad*, had as consorts the *San Antonio*, the *Concepción*, the *Victoria*, and the *Santiago*. The ships were old ones, not in the best condition or fitted as Magellan would have liked. Nevertheless, Magellan—who in 1517 had married Beatriz Barbosa, daughter of an important official in Sevilla—said farewell to his wife and infant son, Rodrigo, before his ships left Sanlúcar de Barrameda on Sept. 20, 1519.

DISCOVERY OF THE STRAIT OF MAGELLAN

The fleet, carrying about 270 men, predominantly from Spain and Portugal but also from far-flung parts of Europe and North Africa, reached Tenerife in the Canary Islands on Sept. 26, 1519, and set sail on October 3 for Brazil. Becalmed off the Guinea coast of Africa, it met storms before reaching the Equator; by November 29, having crossed the Atlantic successfully, it was 27 leagues southwest of Cape St. Augustine (Cabo de Santo Agostinho, Brazil). Rounding Cape Frio, Magellan entered the bay of Rio de Janeiro on December 13. He then sailed south to the Río de la Plata and vainly probed the estuary, seeking the strait. On March 31, 1520, he reached Port Saint Julian (San Julián, Arg.), where on Easter day at midnight Spanish captains led a serious mutiny against the Portuguese commander. With resolution, ruthlessness, and daring, Magellan quelled it: he executed one of the mutinous captains and left another to his fate ashore when, on Aug. 24, 1520, the fleet left Saint Julian.

After reaching the mouth of the Santa Cruz River, near which the *Santiago*, surveying the area, had been wrecked earlier, Magellan started south again. On Oct. 21,

1520, he rounded the Cape of the Virgins (Cabo Vírgenes, Argentina) and at approximately 52°50' S entered the passage that proved to be the strait of his seeking, later to bear his name. The *San Antonio* having deserted, only three of his ships reached the western end of the passage. At the news that the ocean had been sighted, the iron-willed admiral reportedly broke down and cried with joy.

On Nov. 28, 1520, the *Trinidad*, the *Concepción*, and the *Victoria* entered the "Sea of the South," from their calm crossing later called the Pacific Ocean. Tortured by thirst, stricken by scurvy, feeding on rat-fouled biscuits, and finally reduced to eating the leather off the yardarms, the crews, driven first by the Peru Current and throughout the voyage by the relentless determination of Magellan, made the great crossing of the Pacific. Until December 18 they had sailed near the Chilean coast; then Magellan took a course northwestward. Not until Jan. 24, 1521, was land sighted, probably Pukapuka Atoll in the Tuamotu Archipelago (now part of French Polynesia). Crossing the equinoctial line at approximately 158° W on February 13, the voyagers on March 6 made first landfall at Guam in the Mariana Islands, where they obtained fresh food for the first time in 99 days.

A statement sent to King Charles by Magellan before he left Spain suggests that he knew (probably partly from Serrão's letters or perhaps from his own possible voyage there in 1511–12) the approximate position of the Moluccas. In sailing from the Marianas to the islands later called the Philippines, instead of heading directly to the Spice Islands, he was doubtless dominated by the idea of gathering provisions and the advantage of securing a base before visiting the Moluccas. Thus, leaving the Marianas on March 9, 1521, Magellan steered west-southwestward to the Philippines, where, in late March and early April, he secured the first alliance in the Pacific for Spain (at

Limasawa Island) and the conversion to Christianity of the ruler of Cebu Island and his chief men. Weeks later, however, Magellan was killed in a fight with the people of nearby Mactan Island.

CIRCUMNAVIGATION OF THE GLOBE

After Magellan's death only two of the ships, the *Trinidad* and the *Victoria*, reached the Moluccas. Gonzalo Gómez de Espinosa, Magellan's master-at-arms, attempted to return to Spain on the *Trinidad*, but it soon became evident that the ship was no longer seaworthy. Espinosa himself then was arrested by Portuguese officials and imprisoned.

Juan Sebastián del Cano, originally master of the *Concepción* and a participant in the mutiny at Port Saint Julian, took the chance of continuing westward with the *Victoria*, as he likely determined that the crew would not survive another extremely hard voyage across the Pacific. On his way across the Indian Ocean and up the western coast of Africa, he had the chance not to be intercepted by the Portuguese ships that regularly traveled the route. For taking home to Spain, on Sept. 8, 1522, the leaking but spice-laden *Victoria*, with only 17 other European survivors and a small number of Moluccans, "weaker than men have ever been before," Cano received from Emperor Charles an augmentation to his coat of arms—a globe with the inscription "*Primus circumdedisti me*" ("You were the first to encircle me").

ASSESSMENT

Magellan was undoubtedly one of the most skilled sailors of the great age of European maritime discoveries. Yet because he sailed in the service of the king of Spain, Portuguese historians have tended not to grant him the

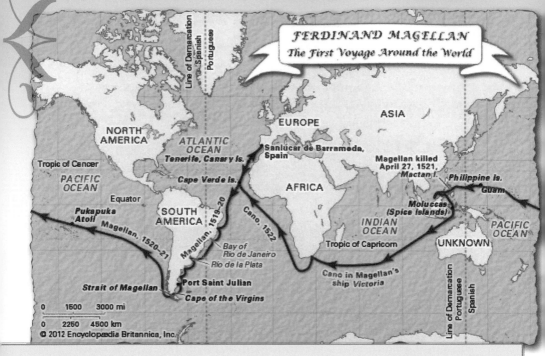

FERDINAND MAGELLAN
The First Voyage Around the World

The first circumnavigation of the globe was led by Portuguese navigator Ferdinand Magellan, who was charged with finding a Spanish route to the Moluccas. He was killed on Mactan Island in 1521, but the expedition returned to Spain under the command of Juan Sebastián de Elcano. Encyclopædia Britannica, Inc.

credit given to other eminent Portuguese navigators, such as Bartolomeu Dias and Vasco da Gama. Spanish historians, on the other hand, have preferred to emphasize the role of the Spanish (actually Basque) navigator Cano. However, Magellan did only what his predecessors Christopher Columbus, John Cabot, and Amerigo Vespucci had done: lacking the opportunity to pursue their goals under the sponsorship of their own country, they looked for support elsewhere. This was a common attitude in the 15th and 16th centuries, a time before the age of nationalism and a time when men pledged allegiance not to the place where they were born but to a king. The early explorers served the monarch who supported their goals of fortune and fame, and the monarch in turn accepted the fealty of men who would enhance the wealth and power of the crown.

Notwithstanding the neglect of Iberian historians, Magellan's complex character, his uncommonly eventful life, and the extreme difficulty of the voyage itself have fueled imaginations ever since the first account of the expedition—recorded by one of its few survivors, Antonio Pigafetta—appeared in the 16th century. Later biographers, such as the 20th-century writer Stefan Zweig, have portrayed Magellan as a symbol of the human capacity to succeed against all odds. Other contemporary authors have attempted to illustrate the magnitude of his accomplishment by likening his voyage through unknown waters to the first explorations of space.

Such a comparison might even be said to underestimate Magellan's feat—a 16th-century maritime expedition was arguably much more unpredictable, and hence far more perilous, than computer-assisted space travel—but in any case, the achievements of Magellan were of profound importance. His supreme accomplishment was the discovery and crossing of the South American strait that bears his name— a major navigational task, considering the knowledge of the period. Moreover, being the first to traverse the "Sea of the South" from east to west, he demonstrated the immensity of the Pacific Ocean and the challenges it posed to navigation. Finally, the idea of the voyage itself had relied on the not-undisputed idea of a spherical Earth. The circumnavigation completed by Magellan's expedition thus confirmed the conception of the world as a globe.

JUAN SEBASTIÁN DEL CANO

(b. c. 1476, Guetaria, Vizcaya, Castile [now Spain]—d. Aug. 4, 1526, at sea)

Juan Sebastián del Cano (also spelled Elcano) was a Basque navigator who completed the first circumnavigation of the Earth.

In 1519 Cano sailed as master of the *Concepción*, one of five vessels in Ferdinand Magellan's fleet, which had sailed west from Europe with the goal of reaching the Spice Islands (the Moluccas) in the East. After Magellan's death in the Philippines in April 1521, a series of men took command of the expedition, but none of them stayed in charge for longer than a few months. As one of the few remaining men, Cano took charge of one of the two surviving ships, the *Victoria*, later that year. He safely brought the expedition home to Spain in September 1522, despite scurvy, starvation, and harassment by the Portuguese. Only 18 Europeans had survived the voyage, which constituted the first journey around the globe.

In 1525 Cano was appointed chief pilot on García Jofre de Loaisa's expedition to claim the Molucca Islands for Spain. The expedition was ultimately a failure, though, and both Cano and Loaisa lost their lives.

CHAPTER 6

MONARCHS AND SPONSORS

The great explorers of the Age of Discovery would not have been able to undertake their expeditions without the sponsorship of certain political leaders, especially Henry the Navigator and King John II in Portugal and Isabella I and Ferdinand II in Spain.

HENRY THE NAVIGATOR, PRINCE OF PORTUGAL

(b. March 4, 1394, Porto, Portugal—d. Nov. 13, 1460, Vila do Infante, near Sagres)

Henry the Navigator (Portuguese Henrique o Navegador)—also known as Henrique, infante (prince) de Portugal, duque (duke) de Viseu, senhor (lord) da Covilhã—was a Portuguese prince noted for his patronage of voyages of discovery among the Madeira Islands and along the western coast of Africa. The epithet Navigator, applied to him by the English (though seldom by Portuguese writers), is a misnomer, as he himself never embarked on any exploratory voyages.

EARLY LIFE

Henry was the third son of King John I and Philippa of Lancaster, the daughter of John of Gaunt of England.

Prince Henry of Portugal, striking a regal pose as a battle victor. His enthusiasm and support for exploration earned him the moniker Henry the Navigator. Hulton Archive/Getty Images

Henry and his older brothers, the princes Duarte (Edward) and Pedro, were educated under the supervision of their parents. Henry emerged with pronounced tastes for chivalric romance and astrological literature, as well as with ambitions to take part in military campaigns and, if possible, win a kingdom for himself.

The starting point of Henry's career was the capture of the Moroccan city of Ceuta in 1415. According to Henry's enthusiastic biographer Gomes Eanes de Zurara, the three princes persuaded their still-vigorous father to undertake a campaign that would enable them to win their knightly spurs in genuine combat instead of in the mock warfare of a tournament. King John consented and, with Ceuta in mind, began military preparations, meanwhile spreading rumours of another destination, in order to lull the Moroccan city into a feeling of false security.

Although a plague swept Portugal and claimed the Queen as a victim, the army sailed in July 1415. King John found Ceuta unprepared, as he had hoped, and its capture unexpectedly easy. Though Zurara later claimed the principal role in the victory for Henry, it would seem that the experienced soldier-king actually directed the operation. That Henry distinguished himself, however, is indicated by his immediate appointment as the king's lieutenant for Ceuta, which did not require his permanent residence there or confer civil authority or administrative responsibilities but did oblige him to see that the city was adequately defended.

An emergency arose in 1418, when the Muslim rulers of Fez (Fès) in Morocco and the kingdom of Granada in Spain joined in an attempt to retake the city. Henry hastened to the rescue with reinforcements but on arrival found that the Portuguese garrison had beaten off the assailants. He then proposed to attack Granada, despite reminders that this would antagonize the kingdom of Castile, on whose threshold it lay. But his father, who had spent years fighting the attempts of the Castilians to annex Portugal, wanted peace with them and sent peremptory orders to return home.

On his return to Portugal, Henry was made duke of Viseu and lord of Covilhã. In 1420, at the age of 26, he was made administrator general of the Order of Christ, which had replaced the crusading order of the Templars in Portugal. While this did not oblige him to take religious vows, it was reported that he afterward resolved to lead a chaste and ascetic life. However, the traditional view of Henry as indifferent to all but religion and the furtherance of his mission of discovery is not supported by later scholarship. Indeed, Henry had not always refrained from worldly pleasures; as a young man he had fathered an illegitimate daughter. Moreover, his brother Duarte, especially after becoming king, did not hesitate to lecture and reprove Henry for such shortcomings as extravagance, unmethodical habits, failure to keep promises, and lack of scruples in the raising of money.

SPONSORSHIP OF EXPEDITIONS

Funds appropriated from the Order of Christ largely financed the Atlantic voyages along the western coast of Africa that Henry began to promote in the mid-1420s. He sought opportunities to take part in the commerce of traditional West African products, especially slaves and gold, and to establish potentially profitable colonies on underexploited islands, the most successful of which he helped to found on Madeira.

Henry's interest in geography unquestionably was influenced by the travels of Prince Pedro, his older and perhaps more brilliant brother. In 1425 Pedro set out on a long tour of Europe on which he visited England, Flanders, Germany, Hungary, and the principalities of Moldavia and Walachia (now Romania) before returning home through Italy, Aragon, and Castile. In eastern Europe he was close enough to Ottoman Turkey to appreciate the Muslim danger. From Italy Pedro brought home to Portugal, in 1428, a copy of Marco Polo's travels that he had translated for Prince Henry's benefit.

Henry's other older brother, Duarte, succeeded King John in 1433. During the five years of Duarte's reign, lack of success in the Canary Islands induced Henry's captains to venture farther down the Atlantic coast of Africa in search of other opportunities. Tradition has claimed that the most important achievement was the rounding of Cape Bojador (now in the Western Sahara) in 1434 by Gil Eanes, who overcame a superstition that had previously deterred seamen. It seems, however, that this is at best an exaggeration, resulting from the vagueness of the sailing directions reported in Portuguese sources. What Eanes mistakenly called Cape Bojador was actually Cape Juby, farther north in Morocco, which had already been passed by many earlier navigators. During the next years, Henry's captains pushed southward somewhat beyond the Rio de Oro. They also began the colonization of the recently discovered Azores, through the orders of both Henry and Pedro.

In 1437 Henry and his younger brother, Fernando, gained Duarte's reluctant consent for an expedition against Tangier. Ceuta had proved an economic liability, and they believed that possession of the neighbouring city would both ensure Ceuta's safety and provide a source of revenue. Pedro opposed the undertaking. Henry and Fernando nevertheless attacked Tangier and met with disaster; Henry had shown poor generalship and mismanaged the enterprise. The Portuguese army would have been unable to reembark had not Fernando been left as hostage in exchange for Henry's broken promise to surrender Ceuta. Fernando's death at Fez in 1443 seems to have been felt by Henry as a grave charge upon his conscience.

King Duarte died in 1438, shortly before Henry's return. His heir, Afonso V, was only six at the time, and Pedro assumed the regency over the bitter opposition of the boy's mother, Leonor of Aragon, who would willingly have accepted Henry as regent. Nevertheless, for most of the next decade Pedro and Henry worked in harmony.

In 1441 a caravel returned from the West African coast with some gold dust and slaves, thus silencing the growing criticism that Henry was wasting money on a profitless enterprise. One of Henry's voyagers, Dinís Dias, in 1445 reached the mouth of the Sénégal (then taken for a branch of the Nile); and a year later Nuño Tristão, another of Henry's captains, sighted the Gambia River. By 1448 the trade in slaves to Portugal had become sufficiently extensive for Henry to order the building of a fort and warehouse on Arguin Island.

Afonso V attained his legal majority at the age of 14 in 1446. His embittered mother had meanwhile died in Castile, and although the young king presently married Pedro's daughter, Isabel, Pedro turned full power over to the youth with obvious reluctance.

Armed conflict between the two became inevitable, and Henry in the end felt obliged to side with the King, though he remained as much as possible in the background. He took no part in a skirmish at Alfarrobeira in May 1449, in which Pedro was killed by a chance shot from a crossbowman. Henry's biographer Zurara, on the other hand, declared that his hero did everything possible to prevent Pedro's death and promised to explain the circumstances further in later writings; but if he did so, the account is lost.

FINAL MARITIME VENTURES

After Alfarrobeira, Henry spent most of his time at Sagres, his castle in the far south of Portugal. He was accorded by the King the sole right to send ships to visit and trade with the Guinea coast of Africa. He appeared occasionally at the Lisbon court and in 1450 helped arrange for the marriage of the King's sister to the emperor Frederick III. During most of his last decade, Henry concentrated on the sponsorship of voyages. These accomplished only minor discoveries, as the Prince now seemed mainly interested in exploiting resources—especially African slaves and, from 1452, the sugar of Madeira—in the regions already contacted. The last two important mariners sent out by Henry were the Venetian explorer Alvise Ca' da Mosto and the Portuguese Diogo Gomes, who between them discovered several of the Cape Verde Islands.

Afonso V had small interest in discovery but great zeal for crusading and knight-errantry. Resuming the old attempt at Moroccan conquest, he led an expedition in 1458 against Alcácer Ceguer (now Ksar es-Shrhir), in which Henry accompanied him. The Prince, now 64, did well in the fighting, and, when the town capitulated, Afonso left the surrender terms to his uncle, who showed remarkable leniency. Henry lived for two years after his return from Alcácer Ceguer.

ASSESSMENT

The farthest point south that was reached during Henry's lifetime was probably present-day Sierra Leone; after his death, the pace of progress in Portuguese exploration accelerated markedly, suggesting that the Prince's reputation as a patron of explorers has been exaggerated. Although the colonization of Madeira proved, at least for a while, to be a brilliant success, most of his enterprises failed. The Canary Islands, the focus of his most unremitting obsessions, eventually fell to Spain, and Portugal did not succeed in garnering much of the African gold trade until more than 20 years after the Prince's death.

His desire to convert the peoples of the Canary Islands and West Africa to Christianity was often voiced but was largely unsupported by action. Nor is Henry's traditional reputation as a champion of the advancement of science supported by any genuine evidence. He did, however, commission chronicles by Zurara that presented a heroic image of himself—an image that persisted for centuries. His long-term importance thus has been as a legendary figure of the early stages of European exploration and discovery, as well as an exemplar of Portuguese nationalism.

JOHN II OF PORTUGAL

(b. 1455, Lisbon, Portugal—d. October 1495, Alvor)

John II, also known as The Perfect Prince (Portuguese O Principe Perfeito,), was king of Portugal from 1481 to 1495. He is regarded as one of the greatest Portuguese rulers, chiefly because of his ruthless assertion of royal authority over the great nobles and his resumption of the exploration of Africa and the quest for India.

EARLY LIFE

John was the great-grandson of the founder of the House of Aviz, John I, and only surviving son of Afonso V by his queen and cousin, Isabella. He was educated by the humanists of the court and was married to his cousin Leonor in 1471. He participated in his father's conquest of Arzila in Morocco, where he was knighted, and was given a separate household at Beja in southern Portugal. In 1474 his father entrusted him with the "trade of Guinea" and the African explorations. When Afonso V claimed the Castilian throne in opposition to Isabella I, plunging Portugal into war, he appointed John his regent (April 1475). The Prince mobilized an army and marched to support his father, but the Battle of Toro (March 1476) checked the Portuguese intrusion into Castile. Afonso V departed for France in a fruitless search for an alliance, while John defended the frontier and parried a Spanish counterattack. Afonso's lack of success caused him to announce his abdication. John was proclaimed king, but his father returned and resumed his reign, concluding the disadvantageous Treaty of Alcáçovas before his death in August 1481.

John II, king of Portugal. King John sponsored exploration of Africa to buoy his county's fortunes via the gold trade. Hulton Archive/Getty Images

ASSERTION OF POWER

At John II's accession, this peace treaty had obliged him to place his young children under Spanish guardianship near the frontier as a pledge of their marriage to Castilians. Afonso had been limited in authority by the ambitious House of Bragança, the wealthiest family in Portugal. John summoned the Cortes (assembly) at Évora (November 1481) and imposed a drastic oath of obedience on his vassals. He also reasserted the *beneplacet,* requiring papal letters to be submitted to him before publication. He successfully negotiated a revision of the treaty with Spain, by which his children were restored to him.

John then accused the Duke of Bragança of treason and had him tried and beheaded at Évora (June 1483). Although evidence was produced that the Braganças had intrigued with Castile, it seems clear that John sought vengeance for their having caused the death of his maternal grandfather, the regent Dom Pedro. He confiscated the Braganças' vast estates and appointed royal judges in what had been private jurisdictions of the nobility. When a second conspiracy sought to remove him and bestow the crown on his wife's brother the Duke of Viseu, John killed his rival with his own hand (August 1484).

AFRICAN EXPLORATION

In Africa Afonso V had preferred crusading in Morocco to trade and discovery of the west coast. John II himself never returned to Africa after Arzila but supported the development of commerce and exploration.

In December 1481 he sent Diogo de Azambuja to build the fortress of St. George at Mina (the "gold mine"), near Benin, a powerful native kingdom in the territory of modern Nigeria. Gold currency had been restored by his father, and the new trade now doubled the royal revenues, and in 1485 John assumed the title of lord of Guinea. He had already sent Diogo Cão to search for the seaway to India, and Cão had discovered the mouth of the Congo River. Christopher Columbus tried to interest him in his plan to reach India by a western route. John rejected this but licensed Fernão Dulmo to search for new islands, apparently without result. In 1485 he sent Cão on a second voyage that reached southwestern Africa but failed to find the Cape. When in 1486 merchants in Benin heard news of a native potentate far to the east who was thought to be the legendary Christian ruler Prester John, the King sent Pêro da Covilhã and Afonso Paiva to visit India and Ethiopia by an overland route. He also sent Bartolomeu Dias to take over Cão's task of finding the southern extremity of Africa; Dias' return in December 1488 demonstrated that Africa could be rounded and India reached by sea, but it was only after John's death that Vasco da Gama's successful expedition to India was launched. In 1490 a mission was sent to consolidate relations with the Kongo kingdom.

In 1493 Columbus arrived in Lisbon with tidings of, as he supposed, islands off Asia, and the Pope awarded these discoveries to the Spanish crown. But John II protested and began negotiations leading to the celebrated Treaty of Tordesillas (June 1494), which gave to Spain all lands west of a line 370 leagues to the west of the Cape Verde Islands. This line, however, reserved Brazil (still apparently unknown) for Portugal.

John had previously negotiated with the papacy, ceding the *beneplacet* but retaining the right to have ecclesiastical cases settled in Portugal and obtaining permission for a crusade against the Moors. He sent a minor expedition against Anafé and obtained tribute from Safi and Azemmour in Morocco, but in 1489 his attempt to build a fortress at the mouth of the Loukkos was prevented by the ruler of Fez.

When in May 1492 Ferdinand and Isabella of Spain decided to expel the Jewish population, John received a delegation of Spanish Jews who offered 60,000 cruzados for the permanent admission of 600 wealthy families to Portugal, together with a fee of eight cruzados a head for the temporary admission of others, who would be allowed to remain eight months, after which John would supply ships for them to leave. In fact, ships were provided only for Tangier and Arzila; some Jewish children were sent to settle the island of São Tomé.

John's son Afonso was married to the eldest daughter of the Spanish rulers, but soon thereafter the Prince was thrown from a horse and killed (July 1491). John was deeply affected. He thought of legitimizing his other son, Jorge, but had already promised the succession to his wife's surviving brother, Manuel. He suffered a long illness and died in 1495 at the small castle of Alvor in the province of Algarve. John's exercise of personal power, particularly against the nobles, explains the epithet the Perfect Prince, which owes its origin to Lope de Vega's play about him.

ISABELLA I OF CASTILE

(b. April 22, 1451, Madrigal de las Altas Torres, Castile—d. Nov. 26, 1504, Medina del Campo, Spain)

Isabella I, also known as Isabella the Catholic (Spanish Isabel la Católica,), was queen of Castile (1474–1504) and of Aragon (1479–1504), ruling the two kingdoms jointly from 1479 with her husband, Ferdinand II of Aragon (Ferdinand V of Castile). Their rule effected the permanent union of Spain and the beginning of an overseas empire in the New World, led by Christopher Columbus under Isabella's sponsorship.

EARLY LIFE

Isabella was the daughter of John II of Castile and his second wife, Isabella of Portugal. Three years after her birth her half brother became king as Henry IV. Despite the fact that she had a younger brother, Alfonso, and that her early years were spent quietly with her mother at Arévalo, Isabella was soon drawn into Castilian politics. She was brought to court when she was 13 in order to be under the king's eye. At first the opposition to Henry IV gathered around Alfonso, but when the latter died in July 1468, the rebellious magnates naturally turned to Isabella. She did not, however, play the role thus designed for her, and the fruit of her wisdom was recognition as his heiress by Henry IV at the agreement known as the Accord of Toros de Guisando (Sept. 19, 1468).

As heiress of Castile, the question of Isabella's future marriage became a matter of increasing diplomatic activity at home and abroad. Portugal, Aragon, and France each put forward a marriage candidate. Henry seems to have wanted his half sister to marry Afonso V, king of Portugal. As between the Portuguese and Aragonese candidates, she herself, no doubt assisted in her decision by her small group of councillors, came down in favour of Ferdinand of Aragon. A third suitor, the French duc de Guiènne, was sidestepped, and without Henry's approval she married Ferdinand in October 1469 in the palace of Juan de Vivero, at Valladolid. The prospect of an Aragonese consort led to the development of an anti-Aragonese party that put forward the claims of a rival heiress, Henry's daughter Joan, known as la Beltraneja by those who believed that her true father was Beltrán de la Cueva, duque de Albuquerque. The king encouraged this group by going back on the accord of 1468 on the grounds that Isabella had shown disobedience to the crown in marrying Ferdinand without

Queen Isabella I of Castile. Christopher Columbus proposed his voyage to the New World to Isabella directly. Stock Montage/Archive Photos/ Getty Images

the royal consent. He now rejected Isabella's claim to the throne and preferred that of Joan, for whom he sought the hand of the duc de Guiènne. Although Isabella and Henry were to some extent reconciled, the long-threatened war of succession broke out at once when the king died in 1474.

REIGN

When Henry died Isabella was in Segovia, which was secured for her claim. She was supported by an important group of Castilian nobles, including Cardinal Pedro González de Mendoza, the constable of Castile (a Velasco), and the admiral (an Enríquez), who was related to Ferdinand's mother. The opposing faction, which put forward the counterclaims of Joan, included the archbishop of Toledo; a former supporter, the master of Calatrava (an influential military order); and the powerful young marqués de Villena. They were supported by Afonso V of Portugal, who hastened to invade Castile and there betrothed himself to Joan. The first four years of Isabella's reign were thus occupied by a civil war, which ended in defeat for her Castilian opponents and for the Portuguese king (Feb. 24, 1479). Upon the death of John II of Aragon in the same year, the kingdoms of Castile and Aragon came together in the persons of their rulers.

Spain emerged as a united country, but it was long before this personal union would lead to effective political unification. Ferdinand, indeed, in his first will (1475) made Isabella his heir in Aragon and openly declared the advantages his subjects would derive from the union with Castile. But each kingdom continued to be governed according to its own institutions. The two sovereigns were certainly united in aiming to end the long process of Reconquista by taking over the kingdom of Granada—the last Muslim stronghold in Spain. In the end, however, the conquest (which began in 1482) proved difficult and drawn out, and it strained the finances of Castile. Although some of the features of the campaign were medieval (such as the order of battle), others were novel. Isabella took a close interest in the conduct of the war and seems to have been responsible for improved methods of supply and for the establishment of a military hospital. In 1491 she and Ferdinand set up a forward headquarters at Santa Fe, close to their ultimate objective, and there they stayed until Granada fell on Jan. 2, 1492.

While she was at Santa Fe another event with which the queen was to become personally associated was in the making, for Columbus visited her there to enlist support for the voyage that was to result in the European settlement of America. Although the story of her offering to pledge her jewels to help finance the expedition cannot be accepted, and Columbus secured only limited financial support from her, Isabella and her councillors must receive credit for making the decision to approve the momentous voyage. The terms on which the expedition was to set out to discover a new route to the Indies were drawn up on April 17, 1492. The New World that was explored as a result of that decision was, with papal confirmation, annexed to the crown of Castile, in accordance with existing practice in regard to such previous Atlantic discoveries as the Canary Islands.

The queen and her advisers hardly needed Columbus to remind them of the opportunity now offered for the spreading of Christianity. Yet the unexpected discoveries quickly brought fresh problems to Isabella, not the least of which was the relationship between the newly discovered "Indians" and the crown of Castile. The queen and her councillors were more ready to recognize the rights of the Indians than was Columbus; she ordered some of those he had brought back as slaves to be released. The

ISABELLA'S JEWELS

In 1484 Christopher Columbus applied to King John II of Portugal for ships and men to probe a sea route west to the riches of Asia. The king's committee decided that his plan was unsound, and the application was refused. Meanwhile, Columbus's wife had died. Taking his son, Diego, he journeyed to Spain to seek backers.

In Spain Columbus made a number of influential friends who helped him present his plan to King Ferdinand and Queen Isabella. Although they were then busy conducting a war against Muslim-ruled Granada, they appointed a commission to examine Columbus's proposal. The commission postponed making a decision, and Columbus was left waiting.

Meanwhile, King John invited Columbus to return to Portugal. Unfortunately, during the second review of Columbus's expedition plan, Portuguese explorer Bartolomeu Dias returned from discovering the Cape of Good Hope at the southern tip of Africa. This meant that an eastern sea route to India was open; the Portuguese were no longer interested in an unproved western route. Columbus returned to Spain. Finally, after the fall of Granada in January 1492, the Spanish sovereigns agreed to finance the expedition. They promised that if he succeeded they would make him admiral of the Ocean Sea and viceroy of all the islands and continents he discovered.

Consortia put together by a royal treasury official and composed mainly of Genoese and Florentine bankers in Sevilla (Seville) provided more than 1,150,000 maravedis (the gold coin of the realm) to outfit the expedition, and Columbus supplied more than a third of the sum contributed by the king and queen. Queen Isabella did not, therefore, have to pawn her jewels to finance the voyage. (This myth was first put about by the Spanish missionary and historian Bartolomé de Las Casas in the 16th century.)

The harbour town of Palos had offended the Spanish rulers, and as a penalty they ordered the town to furnish two ships for Columbus's expedition. These were the *Niña* and the *Pinta*. A third ship, the *Santa María*, was chartered. Columbus commanded this vessel himself and selected two Palos captains to lead the other ships. The crews were recruited in Palos, and the small fleet left port in August 1492.

queen was still concerned with these problems when she died in 1504.

Meanwhile, in 1480 the Inquisition had been set up in Andalusia. There is little doubt that this represented the culmination of a long and popular movement against non-Christians and doubtful converts, which had manifested itself frequently in the late Middle Ages in Castile. The expulsion in 1492 of those Jews who refused conversion was the logical result of the establishment of the Inquisition. Yet, however meritorious the expulsion may have seemed at the time in order to achieve greater religious and political unity, judged by its economic consequences alone, the loss of this valuable element in Spanish society was a serious mistake.

It is difficult to disentangle Isabella's personal responsibility for the achievements of her reign from those of Ferdinand. But, undoubtedly, she played a large part in establishing the court as a centre of influence. With her blue eyes, her fair or chestnut hair, and her jewels and magnificent dresses, she must have made a striking figure. At the same time display was matched with religious feeling. Her choice of spiritual advisers brought to the fore such different and remarkable men as Hernando de Talavera and Cardinal Cisneros. A policy of reforming the Spanish churches had begun early in the 15th century, but the movement gathered momentum only under Isabella and Talavera. When in 1492 Talavera became archbishop of Granada, his place at the queen's side was taken by Cisneros, for whom the monarchs secured the crucial position of archbishop of Toledo in 1495. The monarchs were interested in the reform of the secular clergy and still more in that of the orders of monks, friars, and nuns; Isabella took a particular interest in the reform of the Poor Clares, an order of Franciscan nuns. Although when she died there was still much to be done, the rulers and Cisneros together had gone far toward achieving their goals.

Although Isabella was intensely pious and orthodox in her beliefs and was granted with Ferdinand the title of the "Catholic Kings" by Pope Alexander VI, she could be both imperious and pertinacious in her dealings with the papacy. This was particularly true when she thought the pope was making bad appointments to Spanish benefices or in any way encroaching on the customary rights of the crown over the Spanish churches. For example, for the vacant see of Cuenca in 1478 she rejected the Italian cardinal appointed by the pope, who four years later accepted her alternative Spanish candidate. Subsequently, she successfully rejected the suggestion that the pope's nephew should become archbishop of Sevilla. In seeking to control appointments to Castilian sees, Isabella was not simply inspired by national sentiments. She also sought candidates of high standards; judged by her choices of men such as Talavera and Cisneros, Isabella was remarkably effective in achieving her objective.

Isabella was almost as interested in education as she was in religion. After she reached the age of 30, she acquired proficiency in Latin. At court she encouraged such notable scholars as Pietro Martire d'Anghiera, whom she set up as the head of a new palace school for the sons of the nobility. Naturally, many of the outstanding literary works of her reign, such as Antonio de Nebrija's *Gramática Castellana* (1492; "Castilian Grammar"), were dedicated to her. She was also the patron of Spanish and Flemish artists, and part of her extensive collection of pictures survives.

The last decade of her reign took place against a background of family sorrows brought about by the deaths of her only son and heir, Juan (1497); of her daughter Isabella, queen of Portugal, in childbirth (1498); and of her grandchild Miguel (1500), who might have brought about a personal union between Spain and Portugal. Instead, her daughter Joan, wife of Philip I and mother of the Holy Roman emperor Charles V, became the heiress of Castile. However, this offered little comfort to the queen because by 1501 Joan had already shown signs of the mental imbalance that would later earn her the title of "the Mad."

One of the achievements of Isabella's last decade was undoubtedly the success with which she and Ferdinand, acting on her initiative, extended their authority over the military orders of Alcántara, Calatrava, and Santiago, thus giving the crown control over their vast property and patronage. These orders had been exploited for too long by the nobility and were the subject of intense rivalry among those who sought to be elected master of one or other of them. In 1487 Ferdinand became grand master of Calatrava, and by 1499 he had acquired the grand masterships of Alcántara and Santiago. With the capture of Granada, the main work of the orders had been done, and a process that envisaged their ultimate absorption into the lands of the crown was logical and sensible. Throughout her long reign, Isabella also strove to strengthen royal authority at the expense of the Cortes (Spanish parliament) and the towns.

ASSESSMENT

Good sense and statesmanship were equally reflected in Isabella's will and codicil. Because she left no memoirs, her will is in many ways the most reliable picture of her. In it she sums up her aspirations and her awareness of how much she and Ferdinand had been unable to do. With prudence she comments on the basis of her political pro- gram—the unity of the states of the Iberian Peninsula, the maintenance of control over the Strait of Gibraltar, and a policy of expansion into Muslim North Africa, of just rule for the Indians of the New World, and of reform in the church at home. If the overall impression is inevitably piecemeal, it is also clear that Isabella gave to her succes- sors an exceptional document. It assures scholars that, in allotting to Isabella the foremost place among their rulers, Spaniards do not misjudge this remarkable woman.

FERDINAND II OF ARAGON

(b. March 10, 1452, Sos, Aragon—d. Jan. 23, 1516, Madrigalejo, Spain)

Ferdinand II, also known as Ferdinand the Catholic (Spanish Fernando el Católico,), was king of Aragon and king of Castile (as Ferdinand V) from 1479, joint sover- eign with Queen Isabella I. (As Spanish ruler of southern Italy, he was also known as Ferdinand III of Naples and Ferdinand II of Sicily.) He united the Spanish kingdoms into the nation of Spain and began Spain's entry into the modern period of imperial expansion.

Ferdinand was the son of John II of Aragon and Juana Enríquez, both of Castilian origin. In 1461, in the midst of a bitterly contested succession, John II named him heir apparent and governor of all his kingdoms and lands. Ferdinand's future was assured when he came of age, in

Together with his wife, Queen Isabella of Castile, King Ferdinand II of Aragon initiated a period of exploration and imperialism by the newly unified Spanish nation. Imagno/Hulton Archive/Getty Images

1466, and when he was named king of Sicily, in 1468, in order to impress the court of Castile, where his father ultimately wished to place him. In addition to participating in court life, the young prince saw battle during the Catalonian wars.

John II was careful about Ferdinand's education and took personal charge of it, making sure that Ferdinand learned as much as possible from experience. He also provided him with teachers who taught him humanistic attitudes and wrote him treatises on the art of government. Ferdinand had no apparent bent for formal studies, but he was a patron of the arts and a devotee of vocal and instrumental music.

Ferdinand had an imposing personality but was never very genial. From his father he acquired sagacity, integrity, courage, and a calculated reserve; from his mother, an impulsive emotionality, which he generally repressed. Under the responsibility of kingship he had to conceal his stronger passions and adopt a cold, impenetrable mask.

He married the princess Isabella of Castile in Valladolid in October 1469. This was a marriage of political opportunism, not romance. The court of Aragon dreamed of a return to Castile, and Isabella needed help to gain succession to the throne. The marriage initiated a dark and troubled life, in which Ferdinand fought on the Castilian and Aragonese fronts in order to impose his authority over the noble oligarchies, shifting his basis of support from one kingdom to the other according to the intensity of the danger. Despite the political nature of the union, he loved Isabella sincerely. She quickly bore him children: the infanta Isabella was born in 1470; the heir apparent, Juan, in 1478; and the infantas Juana (called Juana la Loca—Joan the Mad), Catalina (later called—as the first wife of Henry VIII of England—Catherine of Aragon), and María followed. The marriage began, however, with almost continual separation. Ferdinand, often away in the Castilian towns or on journeys to Aragon, reproached his wife for the comfort of her life. At the same time, the restlessness of his 20 years drove him into other women's arms, by whom he sired at least two female children, whose birth dates are not recorded. His extramarital affairs caused Isabella jealousy for several years.

Between the ages of 20 and 30, Ferdinand performed a series of heroic deeds. These began when Henry IV of Castile died on Dec. 11, 1474, leaving his succession in dispute. Ferdinand rushed from Zaragoza to Segovia, where Isabella had herself proclaimed queen of Castile on December 13. Ferdinand remained there as king consort, an uneasy, marginal figure, until Isabella's war of succession against Afonso V of Portugal gained his acceptance in 1479 as king in every sense of the word. That same year John II died, and Ferdinand succeeded to the Aragonese throne. This initiated a confederation of kingdoms, which was the institutional basis for modern Spain.

The events of this period bring out the young king's character more clearly. In portraits he appears with soft, well-proportioned features, a small, sensual mouth, and pensive eyes. His literary descriptions are more complicated, although they agree in presenting him as good-looking, of medium height, and a good rider, devoted to games and to the hunt. He had a clear, strong voice.

From 1475 to 1479 Ferdinand struggled to take a firm seat in Castile with his young wife and to transform the kingdom politically, using new institutional molds partly inspired by those of Aragon. This policy of modernization included a ban against all religions other than Roman Catholicism. The establishment of the Spanish Inquisition (1478) to enforce religious uniformity and the expulsion of the Jews (1492) were both part of a deliberate policy designed to strengthen the church, which would in turn support the crown.

The years 1482–92 were frantic for Ferdinand. In the spring months he directed the campaign against the kingdom of Granada, showing his military talent to good effect, and he conquered the kingdom inch by inch, winning its final capitulation on Jan. 2, 1492. During the months of rest from war, he visited his kingdoms, learning their geography and problems firsthand.

The conquest of Granada made it possible to support Christopher Columbus's voyages of exploration across the Atlantic. It is not known what Ferdinand thought of Columbus or how he judged his plans, nor can it be stated that the first trip was financed from Aragon; the sum of 1,157,000 maravedis came from the funds of the Santa Hermandad ("Holy Brotherhood"). Nevertheless, Ferdinand was present in the development of plans for the enterprise, in the negotiations to obtain the pope's backing for it, and in the organization of the resulting American colonies.

At the age of 50 Ferdinand was an incarnation of royalty, and fortune smiled on him. For various reasons, particularly for his intervention in Italy, Pope Alexander VI gave him the honorary title of "the Catholic" on Dec. 2, 1496. But he also suffered a succession of tragedies: the heir apparent and his eldest daughter both died, and the first symptoms of insanity appeared in his daughter Juana. He was wounded in Barcelona in 1493, but this was unimportant compared with the family injuries he suffered, which culminated in the death of Isabella in 1504, "the best and most excellent wife king ever had."

In 1505, to secure his position in Castile, Ferdinand signed a contract to marry Germaine de Foix, niece of the king of France. This, too, was a political marriage, although he always showed her the highest regard. A stay in Italy

(1506–07) demonstrated how badly he was needed by the Spanish kingdoms. Once more in Castile, he managed his European policy so as to obtain a hegemony that would serve his expansionary ends in the Mediterranean and in Africa. In 1512, immediately after the schism in the church in which the kings of Navarre participated, he occupied their kingdom and incorporated it into Castile—one of the most controversial acts of his reign.

In 1513 Ferdinand's health began to decay, although he was still able to direct his international policy and to prepare the succession of his grandson, the future emperor Charles V. In early 1516 he began a trip to Granada; he stopped in Madrigalejo, the little site of the sanctuary of Guadalupe, where he died. The day before his death, he had signed his last will and testament, an excellent picture of the monarch and of the political situation at his death.

Many considered Ferdinand the saviour of his kingdoms, a bringer of unity. Others despised him for having oppressed them. Machiavelli attributed to him the objectionable qualities of the Renaissance prince. The German traveler Thomas Müntzer and the Italian diplomat Francesco Guicciardini, who knew him personally, compared him with Charlemagne. His will indicates that he died with a clear conscience, ordering that his body be moved to Granada and buried next to that of his wife Isabella, so that they might be reunited for eternity. He died convinced that the crown of Spain had not been so powerful for 700 years, "and all, after God, because of my work and my labour."

CONCLUSION

The motives that spur human beings to examine their environment are many. Strong among them are the satisfaction of curiosity, the pursuit of trade, the spread of religion, and the desire for security and political power. At various times and in particular places, different motives are dominant. Sometimes one motive inspires the promoters of discovery and another motive may inspire the individuals who carry out the search.

These threads are continuous and, being entwined one with another, are difficult to separate. The epic achievement known today as the Age of Discovery was inspired by a combination of mercantile interests, crusading and missionary zeal, and scientific curiosity. During the search for new routes to Cathay, a world new to Europe was found. Discovery was followed by the division of the New World among the great European powers, by the establishment of political, social, and commercial relationships between the New World and the Old, and by the further exploration and mapping of the rest of the globe and the continental interiors. In short, the Age of Exploration led to the delineation of the modern world.

GLOSSARY

annotate To make or furnish critical or explanatory notes or comment to a written document.

bowdlerize To change the content of a written work by omitting or modifying parts considered vulgar.

caravel A small sailing ship of the 15th century, popularly used by explorers of the age.

cartography The study and practice of making geographical maps.

circumnavigate To go completely around something, particularly via a water route.

consecrate To dedicate something or someone to a sacred purpose.

didactic Written or told in such a way that it teaches the reader/listener a moral.

emissary Someone sent to represent someone else.

estuary A section of coastal water that contains fresh and salt water and is partly enclosed by land.

evangelization Of or pertaining to preaching the gospel or converting someone to Christianity.

galley A type of ship or boat that is propelled solely or chiefly by oars.

khan A ruler, often of a Central Asian country.

mangonel A military engine formerly used to throw missiles.

maritime Of or relating to the sea.

Mongol Any of a group of traditionally pastoral peoples of Mongolia.

monsoon A major wind system that seasonally reverses its direction (e.g., one that blows for six months from the northeast and six months from the southwest).

patronage The power to make appointments to government jobs, especially for political advantage.

pension A sum of money paid (as by a government) as a favor or reward for services.

scurvy A disease caused by lack of vitamin C, characterized by loose teeth and bleeding into the skin and mucous membranes.

secular Pertaining to the worldly aspects of public and private life, separate from religious affairs or belief.

shaman A man or woman who has shown an exceptionally strong affinity with the spirit world. Shamans also are considered healers.

sojourn A temporary stay or brief journey.

strait A comparatively narrow passageway connecting two large bodies of water.

sultanate A state or country that is ruled by a sultan, which is a king or sovereign, especially of a Muslim state.

vernacular A language or dialect native to a region or country rather than a literary, cultured, or foreign language.

BIBLIOGRAPHY

THE AGE OF DISCOVERY

Boies Penrose, *Travel and Discovery in the Renaissance, 1420–1620* (1952, reprinted 1975), is still one of the most readable and comprehensive surveys of 15th- and 16th-century European overseas travels. A.P. Newton (ed.), *The Great Age of Discovery* (1932, reprinted 1969), is also a useful overview.

Two scholarly books by a historian of overseas exploration are John H. Parry, *The Establishment of the European Hegemony, 1415–1715: Trade and Exploration in the Age of the Renaissance*, 3rd ed., rev. (1966), and *The Age of Reconnaissance: Discovery, Exploration and Settlement, 1450 to 1650*, rev. ed. (1981). Two books by an eminent American maritime and naval historian that place the Atlantic voyages of exploration in the broader historical context are Samuel Eliot Morison, *The European Discovery of America: The Northern Voyages A.D. 500–1600* (1971, reissued 1993), and *The European Discovery of America: The Southern Voyages A.D. 1492–1616* (1974).

Three classic histories of national overseas expansion are David B. Quinn, *England and the Discovery of America, 1481–1620* (1973); John H. Parry, *The Spanish Seaborne Empire* (1966); and C.R. Boxer, *The Portuguese Seaborne Empire, 1415–1825* (1969). Malyn Newitt, *A History of Portuguese Overseas Expansion, 1400–1668* (2005), is a more recent account.

THE GREAT EXPLORERS AND MONARCHS

Christopher Dawson (ed.), *The Mongol Mission* (1955, reprinted as *Mission to Asia*, 1980), includes information on Giovanni Da Pian Del Carpini and other 13th- and 14th-century missionaries to Mongolia and China. For decades a standard version of Marco Polo's work has been Marco Polo, *The Book of Ser Marco Polo, Venitian*, trans. and ed. by Henry Yule, 3rd ed. rev. by Henri Cordier (1903, reissued in 2 vol. as *The Travels of Marco Polo*, 1993). A modern, readable, and dependable version in English is Ronald Latham (trans.), *The Travels of Marco Polo* (1958), available in many later editions. One of the best studies of Polo, his journeys, his book, and his times is John Larner, *Marco Polo and the Discovery of the World* (1999). Ross E. Dunn, *The Adventures of Ibn Battuta: A Muslim Traveler of the 14th Century*, rev. ed. (2005), is a scholarly though readable biography.

Biographies in English of the early Portuguese explorers are rare and frequently rely on the 16th-century historians João de Barros, Antonio Galvão, and Duarte Pacheco Pereira for historical perspective. A personal narrative written by a member of the Portuguese embassy to Ethiopia in 1520 is Francisco Alvares, *The Prester John of the Indies* , trans. by Lord Stanley of Alderley (1881), rev. and ed. by G.F. Beckingham and G.W.B. Huntingford, 2 vol. (1961, reissued 2 vol. in 1, 1975). Helpful 20th-century works include Eric Axelson, *South-East Africa, 1488–1530* (1940, reprinted 1969); Eric Axelson (ed.), *Dias and His Successors* (1988), on Bartolomeu Dias; and William Brooks Greenlee (ed. and trans.), *The Voyage of Pedro Alvares Cabral to Brazil and India, from Contemporary Documents and Narratives* (1938, reprinted 1967). Sanjay Subrahmanyam, *The Career and Legend of Vasco da Gama* (1997), is a definitive scholarly biography.

Among modern English-language biographies of Christopher Columbus are the classic work by Samuel Eliot Morison, *Admiral of the Ocean Sea: A Life of Christopher Columbus*, 2 vol. (1942, reissued 1962), chatty and discursive but unrivaled in close detail and navigational expertise, also available in a one-volume condensed edition with the same title but lacking the scholarly apparatus (1942, reprinted 1991); Felipe Fernández-Armesto, *Columbus* (1991), arguably one of the best-written and most historically sensitive biographies; and W. Phillips and C.R. Phillips, *The Worlds of Christopher Columbus* (1992). Neiles H. Davidson, *Columbus Then and Now: A Life Reexamined* (1997), caustically reviews disputed points in his career.

John and Sebastian Cabot's voyages are treated in James A. Williamson, *The Voyages of the Cabots and the English Discovery of North America* (1929, reprinted 1971), and *The Cabot Voyages and Bristol Discovery Under Henry VII* (1962, reprinted 1986). A recent biography of Amerigo Vespucci is Felipe Fernández-Armesto, *Amerigo: The Man Who Gave His Name to America* (2007). Luciano Formisano (ed.), *Letters from a New World: Amerigo Vespucci's Discovery of America*, trans. by David Jacobson (1992), is the first English-language compilation of Vespucci's letters and other pertinent documents.

The fullest account of Magellan's remarkable voyage is that of Antonio Pigafetta, who sailed with Magellan and returned with Cano. A recent English edition of this account is *The First Voyage Around the World, 1519–1522: An Account of Magellan's Expedition*, ed. by T.J. Cachey (2007). Laurence Bergreen, *Over the Edge of the World: Magellan's Terrifying Circumnavigation of the Globe* (2003), provides an entertaining account, including detailed descriptions of life aboard the expedition's ships.

All earlier biographies of Henry the Navigator have been superseded by Peter Russell, *Prince Henry "The Navigator": A Life* (2000). John II of Portugal is covered in Elaine Sanceau, *The Perfect Prince: A Biography of the King Dom João II, Who Continued the Work of Henry the Navigator* (1959). Biographies of Isabella I and Ferdinand II include Felipe Fernández-Armesto, *Ferdinand and Isabella* (1975, reissued 1990); and Peggy K. Liss, *Isabel the Queen: Life and Times* (1992)

INDEX